DESIGN FOR AGING
REVIEW

INTRODUCTION BY MICHAEL J. CROSBIE

THE AMERICAN INSTITUTE OF ARCHITECTS
DESIGN FOR AGING CENTER

Published in Australia in 2004 by
The Images Publishing Group Pty Ltd
ABN 89 059 734 431
6 Bastow Place, Mulgrave, Victoria, 3170, Australia
Telephone: +61 3 9561 5544 Facsimile: +61 3 9561 4860
Email: books@images.com.au
Website: www.imagespublishinggroup.com
Copyright © The Images Publishing Group Pty Ltd 2004
The Images Publishing Group Reference Number: 589

Previous editions of this book are:
Design for Aging: 1992 Review (AIA Press)
Design for Aging: 1994 Review (AIA Press)
Design for Aging: 1996–97 Review (AIA Press)
Design for Aging: Four (Published online at www.aia.org)
Design for Aging Review, 5th edition (The Images Publishing Group)
Design for Aging Review, 6th edition (The Images Publishing Group)

National Library of Australia Cataloguing-in-Publication Data

Design for Aging Review, 7th edition.

Includes indexes.

ISBN 1 920744 69 X.

1. Older people – Dwellings – United States – Design and construction.
2. Old age homes – United States – Design and construction.
3. Barrier-free design for older people – United States.
4. Architecture – Awards – United States.
I. The American Institute of Architects Design for Aging Center.

725.560222

Designed by The Graphic Image Studio Pty Ltd, Mulgrave, Australia
www.tgis.com.au
Film by Ocean Graphic Company Limited
Printed by Paramount Printing Company Limited, Hong Kong

IMAGES has included on its website a page for special notices in relation to this
and our other publications. Please visit this site: www.imagespublishinggroup.com

CONTENTS

Assisted Living Facility

Nursing Facility

Senior Living Residence

Special Features

Research Project

Jury Statement

It is an exhilarating journey when four individuals come together for a common purpose with a shared understanding of how the built environment can be meaningful and therapeutic for the elderly. The projects included in this publication represent advances in architecture for the elderly through attention to residents' social and physical well-being, maintenance of community connections, and sound architectural design principles. They illustrate collaboration between the designer and the care provider client, a tenet that is important to both the American Institute of Architects and the American Association of Homes and Services for the Aging, co-sponsors of the Design for Aging Review.

The jury for the seventh cycle of the Design for Aging Review quickly arrived at shared criteria for measuring the projects submitted for consideration. It was critical for projects to have:
- Resident-oriented design solutions
- Environments that enhance the work experience
- Innovation in design and care provisions
- Environments that promote privacy, dignity, and community
- Mission-driven building programs
- Intergenerational connections
- Environments that creatively comply with budgetary restraints

There were eight categories in which the 80 submissions could fall:
- Senior living facilities
- Assisted living facilities
- Special care facilities for those with dementia
- Specialized service or program facilities
- Special features
- Research projects
- Sustainable building solutions

The research project and sustainable building solution categories were new to this cycle of the Review. While the jury was disappointed that no submittals were made in the sustainable building solutions category, we were somewhat encouraged by the submittals in the research project category and anxious to see entries in this category expand in the future.

The number of submittals in the special feature category was above expectations and indicative of two trends—increasing interest in resident-directed wellness and expanded creation of socially oriented, community opportunities within an elderly living campus. Acceptance of the 'household' design concept, with its decentralization and resident orientation, is increasing as well, but more important, designers and clients are demonstrating full comprehension of the goals and benefits of the concept.

The jury wanted each submission selected for inclusion to be one that brings design for the elderly forward through innovation and creativity, and not simply a regeneration of the principles that have worked their way into industry-standard design. We looked with particular interest for projects that responded, through their design, to aspects of senior living that are timeless. These aspects include lifelong learning, healthy aging, intergenerational programming, and resident participation in the provision of care. It was also important that the projects represent a true collaborative effort, with recognition that each team member was critical to the success of the project.

The jury awarded citations, the highest honor, to eight projects for clear and distinct answers to the building program, creative advancement in melding program and environments for the elderly, and demonstrative collaboration among project team members.

As jurors, we understood that the result of our work would be viewed in the future as part of a record of progression in the design for aging. We took our responsibility seriously. As this publication ages and others follow, we hope it will serve as a guide on the journey, showing both where we've been and where we need to go.

Jeffrey W. Anderzhon, AIA
Jury Chair

Design for Aging Review Jury Members

Jeffrey W. Anderzhon, AIA, Jury Chair
Jeffrey Anderzhon is vice president of InVision Architecture and managing partner of the firm's Omaha office, which specializes in design for the aging. He is a member of the advisory group of the AIA Design for Aging Center. He has served on the Architectural Advisory Committee for Iowa State University and the National Program Development Committee for the Assisted Living Federation of America. He served as president of the Alzheimer's Association of Omaha and Eastern Nebraska and as president of the Iowa Chapter of the American Institute of Architects.

Mitch Green, AIA
As managing director of Green Development Management, Mitch Green provides project leadership services to commercial and institutional clients. His more than 25 years of experience in senior housing, healthcare, and commercial facilities began with his MIT master's thesis, 'The Design of Transitional Living Communities for the Disabled,' which won him the AIA Gold Medal. Specializing in healthcare planning and design, Green's completed projects for Brigham & Women's Hospital and the Cottonwood Medical Center won both design and healthcare awards. He pioneered KMD Architects' work in Japan, where his completed projects include an award-winning senior living community in Nagoya and a teaching hospital in Ichikawa. In 1993 Green began eight years as general manager for development of Tokyo's Half Century More Co. He is a membership ambassador of the International Association of Homes and Services for the Aging (IAHSA).

James G. Mertz
James G. Mertz is president and executive director of Asbury Methodist Village, a continuing care retirement community in Gaithersburg, Maryland. Previously he was director of community relations at the Evangelical Lutheran Good Samaritan Society offices, one of the oldest and largest nonprofit skilled nursing and senior housing providers in the United States. Mertz is a Licensed Nursing Home Administrator certified by the American College of Health Care Administrators as an Assisted Living Administrator. He has served on the Housing Committee of the American Association of Homes and Services for the Aging.

Douglas A. Tweddale
Doug Tweddale has been an administrator at Foulkeways in Gwynedd, Pennsylvania, since 1986 and CEO since 1990. Foulkeways is the first Quaker-affiliated continuing care retirement community in the United States. Tweddale has served as director of a hospice home care program and as a family therapist in private practice. He has also served on boards for Friends Services for the Aging and numerous Quaker service organizations.

INTRODUCTION

By Michael J. Crosbie

Design for aging in the U.S. has come a long way since the 1860s, when the classic arrangement of a ward of beds facing a center aisle, monitored by a care-giver, was first established. It became the model of most environments for the elderly for nearly 120 years. This pattern was changed substantially only in the relatively recent past, in the 1980s and 90s, when new designs for the elderly began to emerge. Beyond nursing homes, new types of facilities focused on the total quality of life—physical, social, and spiritual. Assisted living facilities, special care for those with disabilities such as Alzheimer's disease, and continuing care institutions all contributed to a blossoming of new models in design for aging.

Today, as reflected in the projects in this book, there is a wealth of creativity in dealing with the special circumstances of elderly care. These facilities take into account the changing economics of the healthcare market and new attitudes about growing old, sustaining extended families and friendships, accommodating new demands among care-givers, and supporting a sense of community. Selected by a jury of four individuals who are experts in the field, these projects show new directions in design and exemplify environments that promote lifelong learning, healthy aging, programs for people of different generations, and participation of the residents in the provision of care.

Focus on the residents

Perhaps the most important development in design for aging over the past few years has been greater attention to the residents' quality of life. Influenced in part by the boom in 'assisted living' environments, it has had an impact on every level of care, including architecture. The resident has been placed at the center of the care-giving community. The level and intensity of care adjusts as the health of the resident changes. This adjustment can take place in a single facility, which accommodates life changes without the resident needing to leave. Attitudes have changed thanks to the influence of the baby-boom generation, which wants a higher standard of care for its parents (and is now getting a preview of what is in store for them in the next 10 to 20 years).

The focus is on the entire web of associations, needs, desires, and accommodations for the elderly. This includes not only the nourishment of the body, but the mind as well. It brings exercise and fitness to the fore. It includes the spiritual dimension, and the support of family life (accommodated through design). It promotes independence while inviting the residents to make themselves at home.

A typical example of this new emphasis on the quality of life and relationships is seen in new approaches to providing food services. The old model was a regimented system where everyone ate at the same time, and was served the same dish. Today, food service for the elderly offers choice, and caters to the fact that meal times are major opportunities for socializing. Residents want the opportunity to see their meals prepared and served. The Collington Episcopal Life Care Community, for example, offers informal dining rooms, snack bars, and cafés for residents to enjoy depending on their moods and needs. Another project, the Sunset Village Café, is the focal point of a residential community, accommodating those who live there as well as their visiting families and friends. There is a variety of spaces—a formal dining room, a café, a deli counter, and a garden spot for enjoying a meal with others.

The neighborhood connection

One aspect of design for aging now is to find ways to maintain connections between the elderly and their neighborhoods and communities. This allows a more gradual transition from life at home to life in a new community of aging residents. Providing spaces and accommodations for visiting family members and friends allows these connections to flourish and strengthen. More room in resident units for visitors, spaces in the facility for birthday parties and informal friendly gatherings, and proximity to a town center or city, all reinforce this trend.

An excellent example of this approach is Covenant at South Hills in Pittsburgh, Pennsylvania, designed to provide residents with a new home in the heart of the older Mt. Lebanon neighborhood on land provided by a local temple. Existing house forms (older, wood-frame structures) and materials were incorporated into the design to help the facility fit in with the local architectural context.

Another project that extends community life is Avalon Square in Waukesha, Wisconsin, which is a combination of new construction and renovation. Built on an entire block in the downtown core, the building bends around to create a protected courtyard for the enjoyment of the residents. At the corner of Main Street, the façade of a hotel dating from 1871 was preserved as a community landmark, behind which new accommodations for the elderly were constructed. The facility's original 1928 building was also saved and completely updated. The result is a new community for seniors whose connections with downtown —and the neighborhood in which they lived—are accentuated.

A similar approach is seen in California at Sunrise of La Jolla. Constructed on a city block once occupied by a downtown bank building, this 50-unit assisted living facility provides residents with close proximity to busy shops and restaurants. Units along the periphery of the site establish connections with the urban neighborhood, and the upper level offers views of the Pacific Ocean.

Not in my back yard

The flipside of staying in the community is the occasional sourness of established residents whose reaction to the construction of an 'old age home' is simply 'not in my back yard.' According to Jeffrey Anderzhon, who served as the jury chair of this Design for Aging awards program, such resistance is best met by working with the neighbors very early in the project, bringing them along with the design so they feel they are part of the process.

Appropriate architectural responses help new facilities gain local acceptance. The better designs take into account the local vernacular, responding to the scale, massing, materials, and siting of nearby buildings. They are good design neighbors.

Newcastle Place in Mequon, Wisconsin, is an excellent example of this approach. This large project, with more than 80 units, has a scale that suggests a village tucked into the wooded site. Detached carriage homes, combined with community courtyards and wings that appear as large houses, lend the entire facility a comfortable domestic bearing. Most importantly, the architects and other members of the project team worked closely with the neighbors to allay their fears about traffic and falling property values. A well-organized public relations effort featured intensive sessions geared to community education about the project and strong support from local seniors. The result was a sensitively designed project that won the hearts of the neighbors and earned municipal approval.

Two other large-scale projects are domestically scaled and rendered in a style that responds to the local context. La Vida Real in Rancho San Diego, California, is in an appropriate Spanish Colonial style, with massing that suggests a Spanish hill town. Drought-resistant landscaping not only helps to blend the facility with the surrounding neighborhood, but is also a sustainable choice that helps conserve water. On the opposite coast, the Williamsburg Landing, Edgewood Expansion project in Williamsburg, Virginia, is at home in the American Colonial style reminiscent of the original city.

Images of home

Good design not only suggests the familiarity of domestic architecture. The definition of community extends to the very heart of the design. The concept of the 'household' or 'neighborhood' is part of the planning of these facilities, making it easier for residents to identify their new homes within a community of individuals. This trend has been growing for several years, and is now a watchword in design for the aging. The Village at Waveny Care Center in New Caanan, Connecticut, is a clear expression of identifiable neighborhoods within the complex. Each neighborhood comprises 13 rooms focused around a central circulation area, eliminating the need for corridors. All of the neighborhoods have access to communal spaces, some of which recall an old-fashioned downtown street, with shops and eateries and lined with benches and street lamps. The design not only suggests the domestic architecture of the house, but also facilitates the forging of friendships within neighborhoods and a sense of belonging.

Directions for the future

Where is design for aging heading? With increasing costs for healthcare, architects must be more creative in stretching project dollars. Reusing older buildings is one approach. School buildings, apartment structures, and other civic buildings may lend themselves to rebirth as homes for seniors. The jury also noted a trend of modeling new facilities on an older precedent— private homes that became 'old age' homes. While the new facilities offer the latest in care and accommodation, the goal in looking back to the past is to capture the 'homey' feeling of a building originally designed and constructed as a large private home. Solutions inspired by this model are encouraged.

Shrinking nursing staffs pose another design challenge. One approach is to enlist the residents (when they are able) to provide more of their own routine care. This not only lightens the load on the staff, but also fosters autonomy for the resident. Another approach to alleviating staffing shortages is to provide an environment that enhances the work experience, such as amenities and private areas that can be used for breaks.

Realizing the importance of environmental responsibility, the jury anticipates that projects in the future will reflect a greater commitment to sustainable design, construction, and long-term operation. Working with existing site conditions to minimize the impact on the natural environment is one approach. Another is to use sustainable products (those that might contain recycled materials, for example) throughout the facility, and to reduce the building's energy load.

Learning from buildings already in use offers the possibility of research informing the future of design. Research on existing buildings will play a greater role in tomorrow's design, and a 'research' category has been added to the awards program in recognition of this fact. More architects should track the successes and failures of design for the elderly, and incorporate the lessons learned in their designs.

The projects in this volume amply show that architects are up to these future challenges. Inventiveness, creativity, and sensitivity to design—from large-scale planning to intimate details that people can touch—distinguish the architects leading the field.

Michael J. Crosbie is an award-winning architecture journalist and critic, who has authored more than 20 books on architecture.

Continous Care Retirement Community

Community comes together in this urban residence, melding commercial space, creative historic preservation, and a clear urban design language. While the solution is somewhat dense, the interaction of private and public spaces makes the result invigorating. The façade both respects the context and provides a unique sense of place.

Avalon Square

Waukesha, Wisconsin
KKE Architects, Inc.

Architect's statement

Partnering with the city for additional property acquisition, the campus occupies one block, fronting along Main Street in the downtown core area. Integrating the client's existing 1928, five-story building and an 1871 hotel on the historic registry presented a major design challenge.

Avalon Square is a vertically-integrated senior community and mixed-use development offering independent living, assisted living, and a specialty care residence with an emphasis on memory care programming. A full range of opportunities for social, spiritual, and personal activities is offered in the ground level town center. Residents have access to restaurant-style or private dining, a computer-networked activity learning center, chapel, library, museum/art gallery, café deli, convenience store, barber/beauty salon, fitness center, lounges, and a secure landscaped courtyard.

Viable retail space was created on Main Street offering immediate access to additional goods and services, and enhancing the existing urban fabric. The project's scale and use of materials was carefully developed to be sensitive and compatible with the context of the historic downtown.

1

2

3

Site location	Urban
Site area	1.83 acres/80,000 square feet
Capacity	68 apartments; 52 assisted living units; 27 special care for persons with dementia
Total project cost	$22.85 M

1 *Assisted living entry to town center*
2 *Courtyard*
3 *Exterior at Barstow and Main Streets*
4 *Historic Waukesha Hotel*
5 *Gallery*
6 *Independent living entry and retail on Main Street*

Major design objectives and responses

Revitalize a blighted downtown Main Street location

Articulated storefronts, awnings, signage, lighting, hardscape features, landscaping, as well as a recreated hotel loggia were designed to create pedestrian activity and street vitality.

Maintain and integrate the historic 1871 hotel

The structure of the building was dilapidated and unsound, but it was required that the historic hotel remain. It was taken down stone by stone. This stone was stockpiled off-site and then the building was reconstructed with the historically accurate façade and original stone. Research was done to accurately recreate the cupola that had been lost over the years. Large market-rate independent units were designed to work with the building fenestration. A ground level retail space is accessible from Main Street via a loggia that reinforces pedestrian scale along the street.

Integrate the existing Avalon Manor into the CCRC

The existing 1928 building was completely renovated. All units were redesigned with appropriate lighting and current design features while respecting the integrity of the building façade.

Create a design responsive to the multifaceted aesthetics of the site context

The scale of the building is sensitive to the surrounding buildings. The design of the south side of the project takes its cues from the existing 1928 building. Similar forms, fenestration and brick create a referential imagery that is sensitive and complementary to the existing building. The design for Main Street focused on creating a street façade consistent with the existing street edge. Brick, stucco and stone coupled with variations in form break the mass of the project and imply several buildings rather than one.

4

5

6

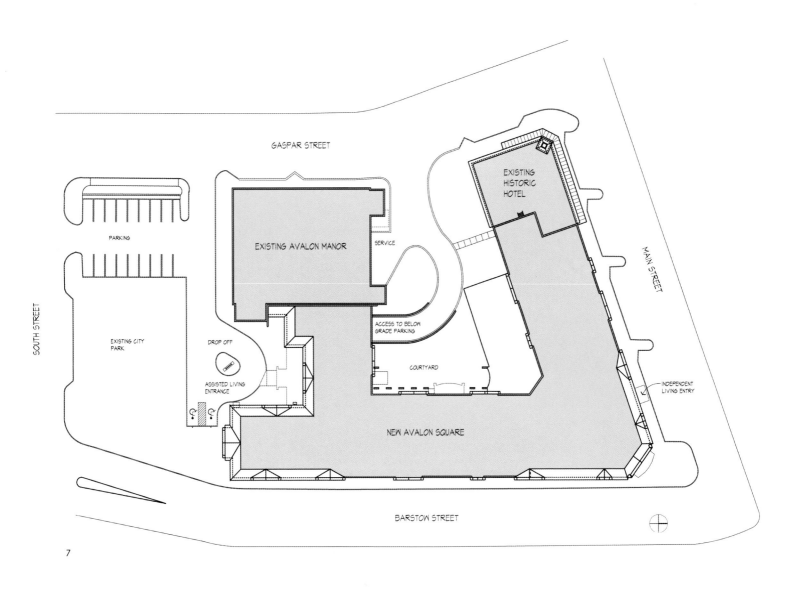

GASPAR STREET

PARKING

EXISTING AVALON MANOR

SERVICE

SOUTH STREET

EXISTING CITY PARK

DROP OFF

ASSISTED LIVING ENTRANCE

ACCESS TO BELOW GRADE PARKING

COURTYARD

NEW AVALON SQUARE

EXISTING HISTORIC HOTEL

MAIN STREET

INDEPENDENT LIVING ENTRY

BARSTOW STREET

7

8

9

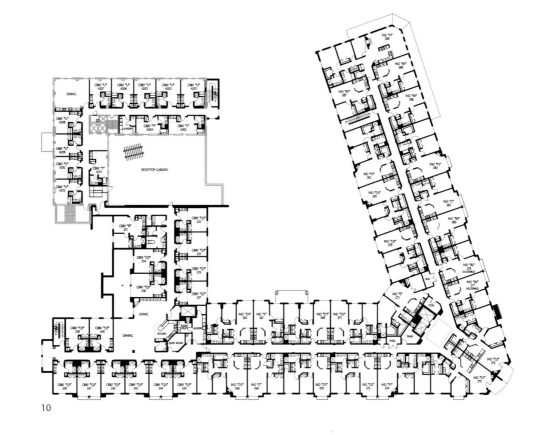

10

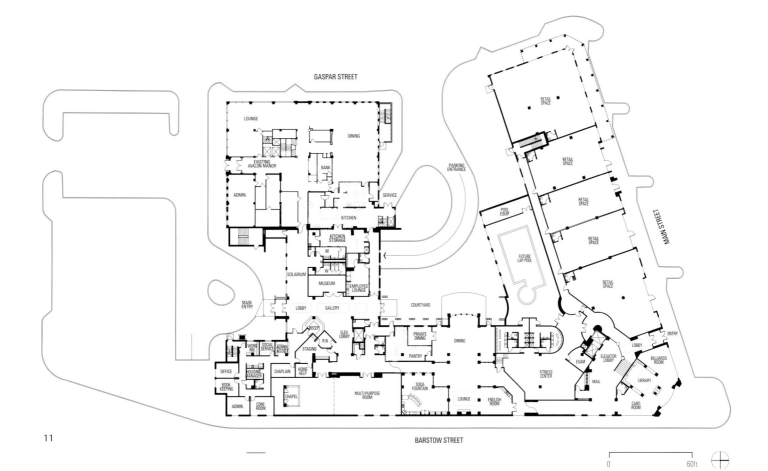

11

12

13

15

14

12 *Dining*

13 *English room*

14 *Fireplace lounge*

15 *Library lounge*

16 *Chapel*

17 *Assisted living unit*

18 *Independent living apartment*

19 *Independent apartment*

Photography: *Philip Prowse*

16

17

18

19

COLLINGTON EPISCOPAL LIFE CARE COMMUNITY MITCHELLVILLE, MARYLAND

Perkins Eastman

Architect's statement

When Collington celebrated its 10th anniversary, the facility faced an uncertain future unless it repositioned itself to meet market demands.

- Older, frailer residents were arriving; couples rejected small units that did not fit their lifestyle.

- The nursing center had shared rooms and medical model operations and environment, and those with dementia had no supportive place to reside.

- Successful fitness, theater, and educational programs outpaced available space, resources, and technology.

More than 40 special interest resident groups met continuously throughout the planning and design process. Community wide presentations and fireside chats with the architects created a unique solution using a thoroughly democratic process.

The repositioned Collington includes large cottages with integral garages, larger garden-style apartments with diverse amenities, a new display cooking dining program, a specially designed environment for dementia residents, a renovated household model nursing center with private rooms, and expanded, upgraded, and reorganized common areas.

1

2

Site location	Suburban
Site area	20 acres/900,000 square feet
Capacity	168 apartment units; 208 cottages/villas; 10 assisted living units; 59 skilled nursing care beds; 34 special care for persons with dementia
Total project cost	$40 M

1   Site plan
2   Building
3   Apartment building addition
4   Adjacent age-restricted condominium community
5   Residential building for residents with Alzheimer's
    and dementia
6   Cottage clusters located above and next to lake

Major design objectives and responses

Consider courtyard views and provide resident orientation cues

The enhanced landscape reinforces the village-like quality of the campus by adding a central focus of new gardens as a 'town square.' The designed landscape spaces create additional opportunities for outdoor informal interaction on campus and have an inviting, lingering appeal. By bringing them to the center of campus and expanding them, the gardens and natural landscape are more accessible and therapeutic.

Offer independence, stimulation, and diverse programs with the comfort and security of full health care services

In addition to the independent lifestyle offered by cottage and apartment living, the design includes a 34-bed facility for persons with dementia. The Arbor offers residents a great room, library, country kitchens, living room, and a safe, secure wandering garden with elevated planters for gardening activities. The dementia program area is now physically and socially integrated into the Collington community, providing a supportive and secure environment.

Offer a choice of living style

The 28 new cottages, each with a patio, are clustered in 11 separate neighborhoods around and above the lake. The two- and three-bedroom cottages offer larger living spaces, garages, covered walkways to the health center, and a variety of floor plans. The apartment building adds 52 new units with a variety of floor plans and larger resident rooms. Community spaces in the apartment building include meeting rooms, wellness, chapel, and game room.

3

4

5

6

8

Opposite   *Formal dining area with display cooking*
8   *Lounge area with bar for socializing*
9   *Country kitchen*

9

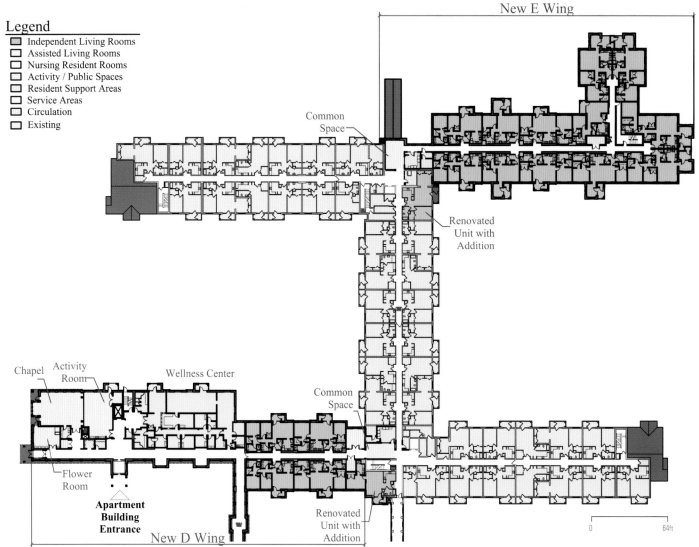

Legend

- ■ Independent Living Rooms
- □ Assisted Living Rooms
- □ Nursing Resident Rooms
- ■ Activity / Public Spaces
- ■ Resident Support Areas
- ■ Service Areas
- ▦ Circulation
- □ Existing

New E Wing

Common Space

Renovated Unit with Addition

Chapel

Activity Room

Wellness Center

Common Space

Flower Room

Apartment Building Entrance

New D Wing

Renovated Unit with Addition

0 ————— 64ft

10

11

12

Legend

- ☐ Independent Living Rooms
- ☐ Assisted Living Rooms
- ☐ Nursing Resident Rooms
- ☐ Activity / Public Spaces
- ☐ Resident Support Areas
- ☐ Service Areas
- ☐ Circulation
- ☐ Existing

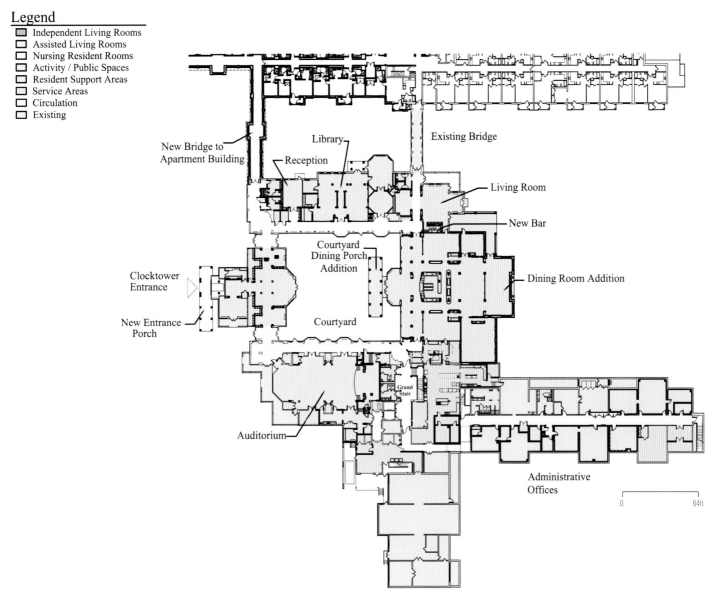

New Bridge to Apartment Building

Library

Reception

Existing Bridge

Living Room

New Bar

Clocktower Entrance

Courtyard Dining Porch Addition

Dining Room Addition

New Entrance Porch

Courtyard

Grand Stair

Auditorium

Administrative Offices

0   64ft

13

14

10   *Apartments, typical floor plan*

11   *Apartment living room*

12   *Apartment bedroom*

13   *Community center floor plan*

14   *Dementia building living room*

Photography: *Massery Photography*

Lasell Village

Newton, Massachusetts

Steffian Bradley Architects

Architect's statement

Lasell Village consists of 162 independent living units with 14 buildings connected through a network of glass-enclosed walkways and bridges. Two campuses were formed consisting of seven buildings each, surrounding a village square reminiscent of typical New England villages. Wide connecting corridors of the Village 'Town Hall' form an interior Main Street.

The 13 residential buildings all contain varied seminar rooms to support the unique Lifelong Learning Program. As a condition of residence, villagers must participate in 450 hours of continued education per year. Classroom functions include lecture rooms, reading/library rooms, computer room, art studio, gardener's room, exercise room and indoor pool. Off-campus learning activities are also part of the curriculum.

1

2

3

Site location	Suburban
Site area	13.2 acres
Capacity	162 units; 44 skilled nursing care beds
Total project cost	Owner withheld

4

5

Major design objectives and responses

Create indoor and outdoor spaces that encourage interaction and community

All buildings are connected through a network of glass-enclosed walkways and bridges. A Town Hall building forms a central meeting place, offering outdoor gardens and terraces, dining options, a wellness center, bank office, ballroom, research offices and a 44-bed skilled nursing facility. Connecting walkways and corridors of the Town Hall widen to form an interior village square at their intersection. Residents can travel between buildings indoors through connecting walkways, bridges and elevators.

Relate to the surrounding 19th-century neighborhood and college buildings

The campus plan with the Town Hall as the focal point of the site harkens back to many New England college campuses. The order and formality of the two campus quadrangles are juxtaposed with gently meandering driveways and paths.

Establish comfortable residential buildings with a human scale and abundant natural light

The use of larger than normal horizontal siding, and generous windows help make these buildings appear smaller and more human-scaled to the residents. Enclosed walkways consist of patio doors that bring natural light and ventilation into the corridors, maintain a connection to the surrounding landscape, and provide spatial orientation within the community.

Establish a cohesive language among buildings on the campus

This was accomplished by utilizing architectural forms such as symmetrical double masonry gables at points of entrance and dormers which define roof lines, plus beautifully detailed bridges that span the central drive and serve as arched gateways to the north and south campuses.

6

7

1   Town Hall building
2   Residential building
3   Interior village town square
4   Connecting bridge forms entry gateway
5   Site plan
6   Dormers reduce mass of residential buildings
7   Enclosed walkway links campus buildings
Photography: *Dimitri Papadimitriou*

SUN CITY TAKATSUKI

TAKATSUKI, JAPAN

Perkins Eastman / Associate architect: Kanko Kikaku Sekkeisha

Architect's statement

Though a large building, the program elements are scaled to fit comfortably into a neighborhood of single-family homes. Independent living senior apartments flank the entry court to the north, while a U-shaped house to the south provides dementia care, skilled nursing, and assisted living options on each of its three floors. Completed in September 2001, the $32 million, 170,000-square-foot facility incorporates 24 assisted living units, 91 independent living units, and 68 specialized nursing/dementia units. These residential environments are connected through the idea of an interior street or promenade lined with social spaces that link the small-scale neighborhoods.

1

2

Site location	Suburban
Site area	4.7 acres/170,000 square feet
Capacity	91 apartments; 24 assisted living apartments; 34 special care for persons with dementia; 34 skilled nursing care beds
Total project cost	$32 M

Major design objectives

One of the first retirement communities of its kind in Japan, Sun City Takatsuki:

- Represents the challenge of creating retirement living in a country with no tradition of senior living.
- Bridges the cultural divide between western programs and insights and Japanese family traditions and culture.
- Serves Japan's rapidly aging population in a contemporary, high service and hospitality-like setting.

1   Interior courtyard
2   Entry court and canopy
3   Units offering mountain views
4   Southeast exposure
5   Library at dusk

3

4

5

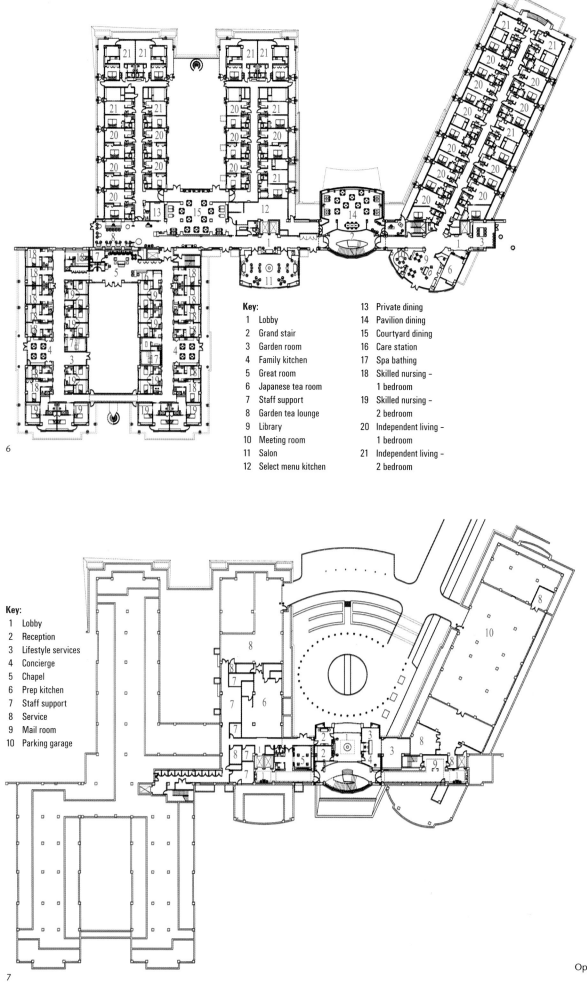

Key:

1 Lobby
2 Grand stair
3 Garden room
4 Family kitchen
5 Great room
6 Japanese tea room
7 Staff support
8 Garden tea lounge
9 Library
10 Meeting room
11 Salon
12 Select menu kitchen

13 Private dining
14 Pavilion dining
15 Courtyard dining
16 Care station
17 Spa bathing
18 Skilled nursing –
   1 bedroom
19 Skilled nursing –
   2 bedroom
20 Independent living –
   1 bedroom
21 Independent living –
   2 bedroom

6

Key:

1 Lobby
2 Reception
3 Lifestyle services
4 Concierge
5 Chapel
6 Prep kitchen
7 Staff support
8 Service
9 Mail room
10 Parking garage

7

6   *First floor plan*

7   *Ground floor plan*

Opposite   *Staircase*

9

10

9 Casual dining

10 Formal dining

11 Library

12 Private resident room

13 Garden tea lounge

Photography: *Chuck Choi Architectural Photography*

11

13

12

BROOKSBY VILLAGE, PHASE 1

PEABODY, MASSACHUSETTS
Steffian Bradley Architects

Architect's statement

Brooksby Village provides housing and health services for middle-income seniors—the first of its kind in New England. With two of three phases now complete, the entire campus will contain 1,350 units of independent housing in addition to 190 assisted living and 320 skilled nursing beds.

The design concept is to create a community modeled after traditional New England villages; buildings are clustered around a unifying town hall facility to create three individual neighborhoods. Each neighborhood consists of two to five residential apartment buildings, a multifunction community building, pathways, and courtyards. This vibrant campus is linked via an extensive system of climate-controlled walkways and an active main street.

Several design challenges arose from the site's prior use as a landfill, zoning criteria, and wetland setbacks. The responsive design respects existing vegetation and land features, situating Brooksby Village comfortably into its surrounding environment.

1   Neighborhood One across the restored path
2   Neighborhood One courtyard and enclosed pool
3   Community building 1.0 plan: second floor
4   Community building 1.0 plan: first floor
5   Lobby
Photography: John Coletti

1

2

Site location	Suburban
Site area	14.9 acres/650,000 square feet (Neighborhood One)
Capacity	525 units (Neighborhood One)
Total project cost	Owner withheld

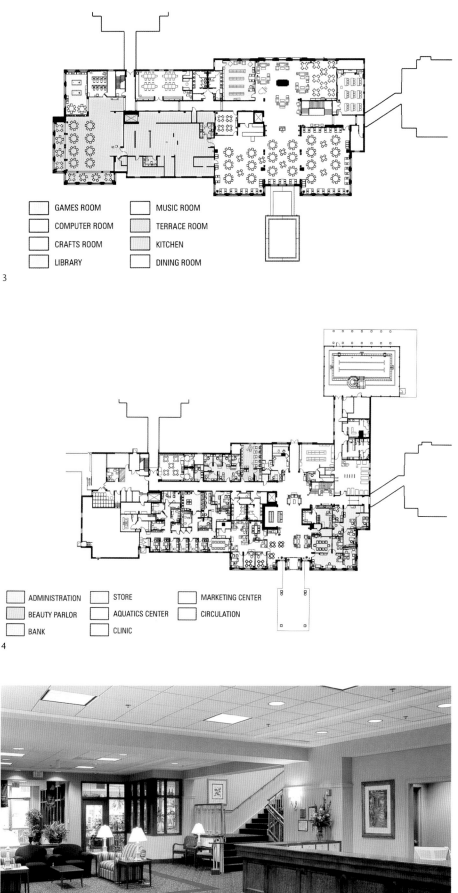

GAMES ROOM
COMPUTER ROOM
CRAFTS ROOM
LIBRARY

MUSIC ROOM
TERRACE ROOM
KITCHEN
DINING ROOM

3

ADMINISTRATION
BEAUTY PARLOR
BANK

STORE
AQUATICS CENTER
CLINIC

MARKETING CENTER
CIRCULATION

4

5

Major design objectives and responses

Establish a strong sense of community within a residential development

This project was modeled after the quadrangles of university campuses. Clusters of mid-rise residential buildings surround a central community building and a courtyard to form distinct individual neighborhoods. These apartment neighborhoods are linked via covered walkways and an interior main street that connects all areas of the campus. Community buildings serve as the hub of each neighborhood and perform functions similar to that of a town hall of historic New England villages.

Encourage a healthy and active lifestyle for residents

As seasons can impair year-round activity, the design team linked every building with climate-controlled covered walkways and bridges. Residents can enjoy walks through courtyards or seek entertainment and recreation offered at the community buildings. Facilities include a health club and aquatic center, and medical and pharmaceutical needs are also provided for.

Engage and respect the existing environment and natural surroundings

Existing boulders were used as landscape features, while existing gravel mounds create varied topography in many of the courtyards. Each residential neighborhood's courtyard was given a distinct identity and theme. To welcome residents into their natural surroundings, walking trails wind throughout the landscape.

Create a variety of scale and spatial relationships, giving the campus a residential feel

Bay windows and porches provide differentiation and pitched roofs create visual interest where the buildings meet the sky, referencing the iconic expression of home. While apartment buildings range in height from five to seven stories, the community buildings are only two stories, adding more variation within each neighborhood. The massing of the second neighborhood is reduced in scale to mediate between the larger-scaled neighborhoods on either side and the natural beauty of the wooded slope at its backdrop.

Covenant at South Hills

Pittsburgh, Pennsylvania

Cochran, Stephenson & Donkervoet, Inc. / Associate architect: Rothschild Architects

Architect's statement

The project is situated in an area of Pittsburgh characterized by large homes, long-term family ownership and commitment to community, and a large, diverse, and highly educated predominantly reformed Jewish community.

The project rests on an extremely steep site that presented many design challenges to the owner and design team. The site has virtually no street visibility, and was originally part of the property owned by the temple at the top of the site. The site dictated a solution that worked with the hillside, accommodated adequate parking, and would allow for separate buildings for independent living, assisted living, skilled nursing, and commons. The project was designed to provide residents with a new home in the heart of the Pittsburgh area, by looking to the existing housing forms and materials (stone, siding, and brick) for inspiration.

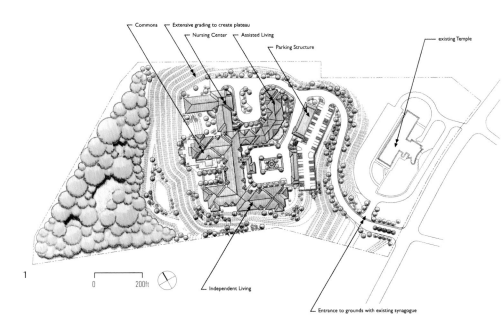

1

2

3

Site location	Suburban
Site area	15 acres/668,400 square feet
Capacity	126 apartments; 48 assisted living units; 12 special care for persons with dementia; 46 skilled nursing care beds
Total project cost	Not known

Commons Plan

The Commons creates a sense of "home" with features including a fire place, intimate sitting areas and private dining room.

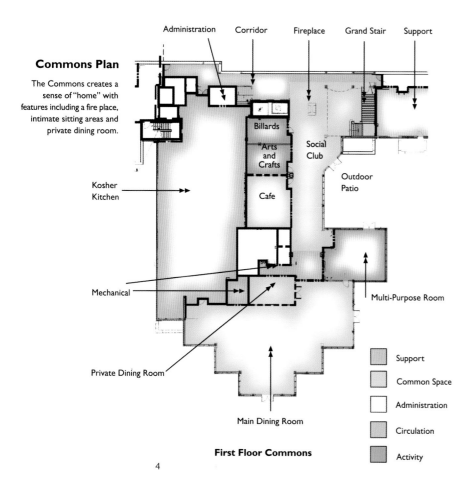

First Floor Commons

4

- Support
- Common Space
- Administration
- Circulation
- Activity

Labels: Administration, Corridor, Fireplace, Grand Stair, Support, Billards, Arts and Crafts, Social Club, Outdoor Patio, Kosher Kitchen, Cafe, Mechanical, Multi-Purpose Room, Private Dining Room, Main Dining Room

5

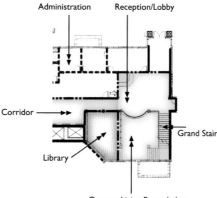

Second Floor Entry/Lobby/Commons

6

Labels: Administration, Reception/Lobby, Corridor, Grand Stair, Library, Open to Living Room below

1 Site plan
2 Outdoor dining
3 Independent apartments
4 Commons first floor plan
5 Exterior
6 Commons second floor plan
Photography: Alain Jaramillo

Major design objectives and responses

Link the residents to their current lifestyle in Mt. Lebanon

The project transformed a site that at first seemed to pose significant challenges into a compact and high quality project for its residents. Adjusting the project to this site allowed the project to stay in Mt. Lebanon rather than move to another location outside the center of Jewish life in the South Hills.

Relate to the existing neighborhood

Through imagery of the existing housing and materials, the projects used a similar palette of materials to render a fairly large and compact building to be as residential and homelike as possible.

Attract the Jewish community to the project without excluding everyone else in the market

These issues were often debated, and in some cases changed right up to the final documents. The kitchen went from a kosher-style solution to a strict kosher kitchen during working drawings. This necessitated the addition of another cooking line and additional storage.

For the potential resident and visitor to understand the site and building solution upon entering

The skilled nursing facility and assisted living have their own entry court physically separate from the independent living entrance.

Community functions to be incorporated so they are obvious to the user

The stacking of the community spaces beneath the independant wings makes the use of the two-story lobby and grand stair critical in linking the function spaces to the front door and the bulk of the units.

EDGEMERE

DALLAS, TEXAS
three

1

Architect's statement

Reminiscent of a period Tuscan village, the project marries old with new by incorporating the design of an eighteenth-century Italian village with modern steel and concrete construction. Large in scope yet intimate in scale, the project is a CCRC for more than 400 senior residents. The progression of interior spaces is organized around a major common area spine, which is independent of the service functions. Asymmetry is prevalent throughout, reinforcing the concept of a building that has evolved over time. Through careful articulation of the building masses and variation of the elevation elements, the design team has composed a variety of distinctive spaces, all of which are tailored to the senior lifestyle.

The owner wanted to make all areas of the two-story commons building inviting so that the residents would venture into these areas and enjoy them. The team accomplished this by creating areas with interesting curves, twists and turns, niches, and fountains while also utilizing those features for senior wayfinding.

2

Site location	Urban
Site area	15.47 acres/673,873 square feet
Capacity	259 apartments; 60 assisted living units; 45 special care for persons with dementia; 66 skilled nursing care beds
Total project cost	Not available

1   Independent living building entry
2   Sculpture court over garage
3   Independent living apartments
4   Balcony detail
5   Dining court

Major design objectives and responses

Attractive to potential market
Old world Tuscan architecture.

Create attractive views from all units
Buildings were arranged to create interior courtyards.

Minimize car visibility
Underground parking.

Provide first class amenities
Larger and more opulent common area.

Respond to the competition
Attention to detail.

3

4

5

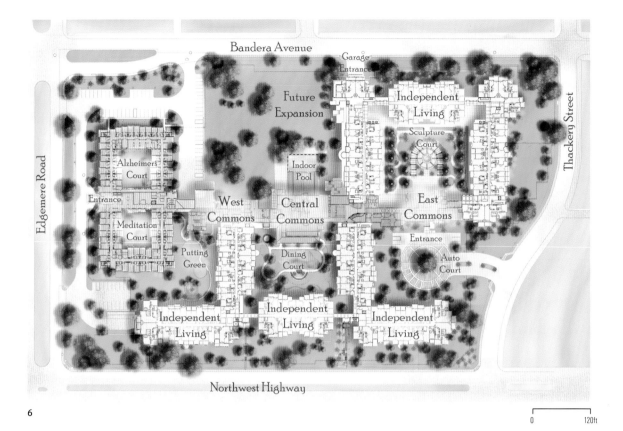

Bandera Avenue

Garage Entrance

Future Expansion

Independent Living

Sculpture Court

Indoor Pool

Alzheimers Court

Entrance

Meditation Court

West Commons

Central Commons

East Commons

Putting Green

Dining Court

Entrance

Auto Court

Independent Living

Independent Living

Independent Living

Edgemere Road

Thackery Street

Northwest Highway

6

0   120ft

Indoor pool

Parking garage

Fitness

Staff

Main kitchen

Private dining

Billiards

Atrium

Dining room

Dining arcade

7

0   40ft

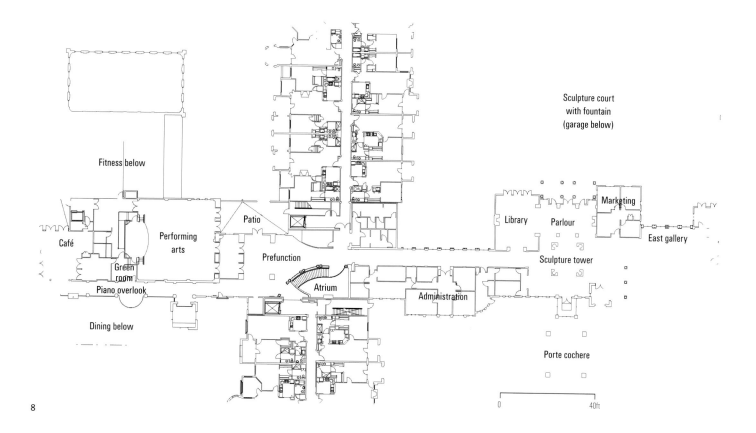

Fitness below

Sculpture court
with fountain
(garage below)

Café

Performing
arts

Patio

Green
room

Prefunction

Piano overlook

Atrium

Dining below

Administration

Marketing

Library

Parlour

East gallery

Sculpture tower

Porte cochere

0   40ft

8

9

10

11

14

13

12 *Commons foyer*
13 *Commons parlor*
14 *Indoor pool*
Photography: *Craig Blackmon, AIA (10,11,13);*
Grant Warner (1–5,9,12,14)

EPISCOPAL CHURCH HOME

MEMORY CARE CENTER OF EXCELLENCE LOUISVILLE, KENTUCKY

Reese Design Collaborative, PSC

Architect's statement

The challenge was to provide individual residences for 52 persons and a community space for 250 existing residents plus family members. The design solution was de-institutionalized through development of a residential scale, both on the exterior and interior, reminding the residents of the homes they once knew.

The two neighborhood buildings each contain four uniquely identifiable houses. Each house emphasizes traditional living and dining functions, including either six or seven bedrooms with bath. Care-giver support areas are seamlessly integrated within each kitchen. Service support is provided through concealed access to each living area and, except for food delivery, is completed at night.

The community space is fashioned to represent a mall, including a large, two-story skylit rotunda, which serves as a central gathering and circulation center. A variety of shops and meeting spaces offer all residents and family members a variety of interactive experiences.

1

2

3

Site location	Suburban
Site area	7.52 acres/372,554 square feet
Capacity	36 cottages/villas; 75 assisted living units; 52 special care for persons with dementia; 139 skilled nursing care beds
Total project cost	$8.06 M

1 *Distinct porch assists wayfinding*

2 *Covered porch, gazebo, planting areas, and walking path*

3 *Exterior*

4 *Project site plan*

Major design objectives and responses

Reflect resident centered, resident directed care

Care-giving requirements were disguised within the desired residential setting. Residents can sit comfortably at a low counter in a central kitchen shared by two houses, and when lying in bed, the bathroom and toilet are in their direct line of sight.

Incorporate key principles of the Eden Alternative™ by creating a human habitat

The inclusion of animals, plants, a diversity of useable spaces, and a variety of styles were all key considerations. Beginning in the mall, a pet shop, complete with outdoor respite location was developed. An adjacent flower shop offers fresh flowers to be arranged by residents as well as seeds and supplies for use in the variety of gardens. Aviaries and aquariums have been strategically located to attract residents' attention, while providing a sense of comfort, entertainment, and companionship.

Attract people to public points of interest to create interaction

Each shop in the mall creates its own unique opportunity to meet, celebrate, and enjoy the company of others. The rotunda becomes a festive venue for parties and other celebrations, while the soda fountain's jukebox and popcorn machine lure passersby into spontaneous gatherings.

De-institutionalize the architecture and scale of the facility

Elements of a typical house are carefully integrated through the use of traditional brick exterior façades, with comfortably scaled windows, clerestory copulas, sunrooms, screened porches and courtyards. Interior circulation routes are carefully defined to separate resident use from service use.

Freedom of movement within protected perimeter

Upon entering each neighborhood building, residents have full, unrestricted movement, as well as three uniquely different courtyards with these exterior spaces becoming the remote point of control.

4

0   30ft

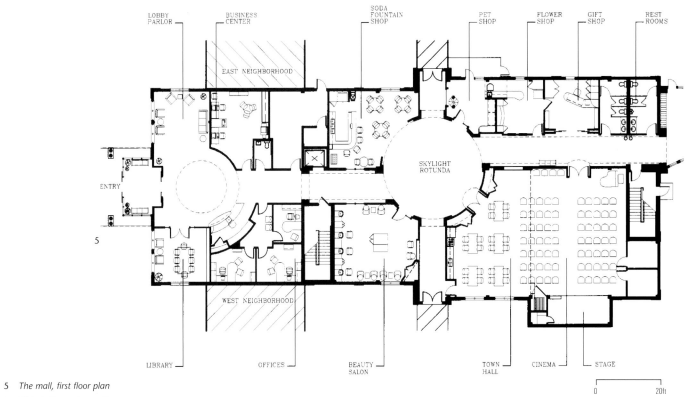

Labels on floor plan:

LOBBY PARLOR — BUSINESS CENTER — SODA FOUNTAIN SHOP — PET SHOP — FLOWER SHOP — GIFT SHOP — REST ROOMS

EAST NEIGHBORHOOD

ENTRY

SKYLIGHT ROTUNDA

5

WEST NEIGHBORHOOD

LIBRARY — OFFICES — BEAUTY SALON — TOWN HALL — CINEMA — STAGE

0   20ft

5   *The mall, first floor plan*

6   *Main lobby and reception area*

7   *The mall*

6

7

8

9

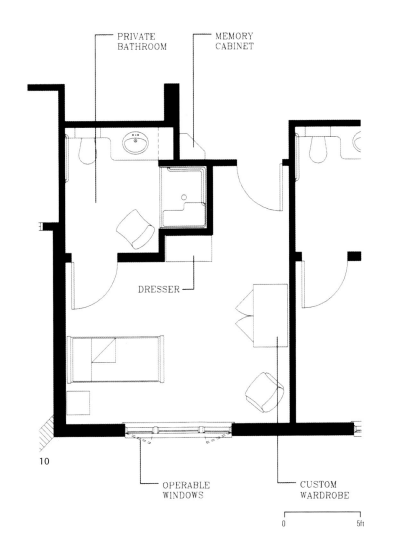

PRIVATE BATHROOM | MEMORY CABINET

DRESSER

10

OPERABLE WINDOWS | CUSTOM WARDROBE

0   5ft

8 Soda fountain shop

9 Shared dining room and kitchen area

10 Resident room floor plan

11 River-themed living room

12 Old Louisville-themed living room

Photography: Bryan Moberly Photography

11

12

Friendship Village of Schaumburg

Schaumburg, Illinois

Dorsky Hodgson + Partners, Inc. / Associate architect: Jaeger Nickola Associates

Architect's statement

The key objective of the design program was to reposition this 1977 CCRC for the future.

The design response is a series of additions and demolitions developed through a decision-making planning matrix aligned with the community's strategic plan. Task force groups, focusing on the key design directives, provided a participatory process that engaged all stakeholders.

The lakefront site, the covered arcade, and outdoor garden linking the lifestyle center and the spiritual center emphasize a harmony with nature and the client's philosophy of connectedness, and their holistic approach to wellness. The architectural design is contemporary; the interior architecture is modern; natural light is incorporated throughout the design and is used as an orienting element; the new two-story Winter Garden is an architectural element that links the new building to the existing buildings, and is reminiscent of the atrium remaining in the existing building.

1

Site location	Suburban
Site area	16.5 acres/718,740 square feet
Capacity	170 apartments;
	28 cottages/villas
Total project cost	$59 M

2

3

4

Major design objectives and responses

Create a new entry
The new building is located in view from the entry drive and required careful site planning to fit between an existing building and the lake.

Strengthen connections between the interior and exterior and create meaningful exterior spaces
The Winter Garden is a two-story space that slices through the entry providing a link that connects multiple interior spaces and several outdoor gardens.

Segregate back-of-house service functions from resident areas
Service connections between the buildings are provided at the lower garage level. Separate service entries and existing building links are designed for each phase.

Demolish some of the most deficient existing buildings in order to grow and meet the design objectives, and phase construction to accommodate all residents
The very tight site required extensive scenario planning to create a feasible build and demolish sequence.

Provide choice and flexibility in housing and service options
The phase I garden homes provide a new independent housing option in a single-story cluster housing design. The phase II building is six stories and 170 units with underground parking. In addition to the new option of larger apartment suites, the design includes 56,000 square feet of community space, providing multiple dining options and several meeting and creative expression areas. It also includes a classroom, a resource center, a formal and informal gathering space and a complete wellness/lifestyle center including an aquatic center and spa.

1   Lake Shore building; lake view
2   Garden home quartet plan
3   Lake Shore building; entry view
4   Aquatic center

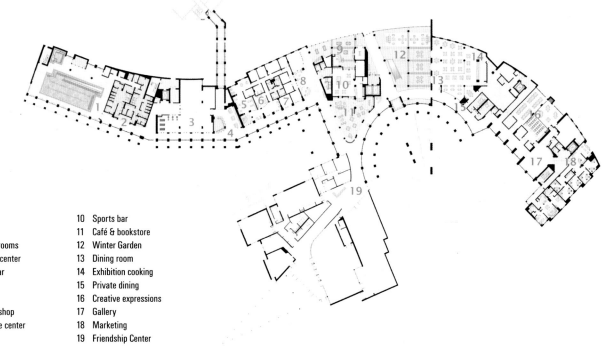

Key:

1	Pool	10	Sports bar
2	Locker rooms	11	Café & bookstore
3	Fitness center	12	Winter Garden
4	Juice bar	13	Dining room
5	Salon	14	Exhibition cooking
6	Spa	15	Private dining
7	Barber shop	16	Creative expressions
8	Lifestyle center	17	Gallery
9	Retail	18	Marketing
		19	Friendship Center

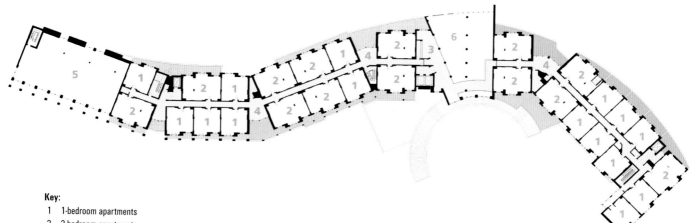

Key:

1   1-bedroom apartments
2   2-bedroom apartments
3   Mezzanine lounge
4   Resident lounge
5   Open to pool below
6   Open to Winter Garden below

7

5   *Ground floor; community spaces*
6   *Winter Garden view toward entry*
7   *Second floor plan; resident suites*
8   *Dining room with exhibition kitchen*
9   *Exhibition kitchen elevation*

Renderings: *DORSKY HODGSON + PARTNERS, Inc.,*
Anderson Illustration, Inc.

8

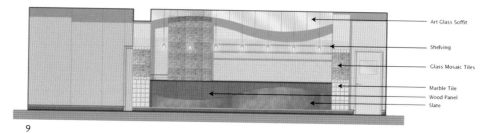

Art Glass Soffit

Shelving

Glass Mosaic Tiles

Marble Tile
Wood Panel
Slate

9

THE GARLANDS OF BARRINGTON

BARRINGTON, ILLINOIS

Torti Gallas and Partners • CHK, Inc

Architect's statement

Set within an existing park-like setting, The Garlands of Barrington is a campus of buildings and gardens designed as an intergenerational neighborhood addition to the Village of Barrington. Fundamental to the design is the desire to create meaningful public open spaces and gardens that will draw the community onto the site and provide numerous opportunities for outdoor activities. Inviting walking paths in landscaped gardens encourage both resident and public usage. In addition, the design incorporated a mix of restaurants, outdoor cafés, and general retail, as well as spa and fitness centers that are open for public and resident use.

Located on the former American National Can Company facility site, The Garlands at Barrington is the finest continuing care retirement community in the Chicago area. Here residents will own and enjoy fine homes and have the peace of mind of having service and care for life, all in close proximity to the Barrington Village downtown shopping centers, restaurants, churches, medical offices, and public library.

1

1&2   Independent living units
   3   Porte-cochere at independent
        living units
   4   View of new villas
   5   Exterior detail
   6   Exterior detail of villas

Site location	Suburban
Site area	31.5 acres
Capacity	271 apartments; 26 villas; 69 assisted living units; 20 special care for persons with dementia; 19 skilled nursing care beds
Total project cost	$157.2 M

2

3

Major design objectives and responses

Give the community exterior spaces that have a natural park-like setting and campus feel
Place the majority of parking beneath the buildings, reduce on-grade paving, preserve existing green space and trees.

Create a community based on traditional urban design principals where residences and amenities are within walking distance
Buildings are clustered tightly around a walking path network between dwellings and services.

High quality traditional architecture
Develop a Northern European style of architecture to complement and blend with the current style of Barrington Village.

4

5

6

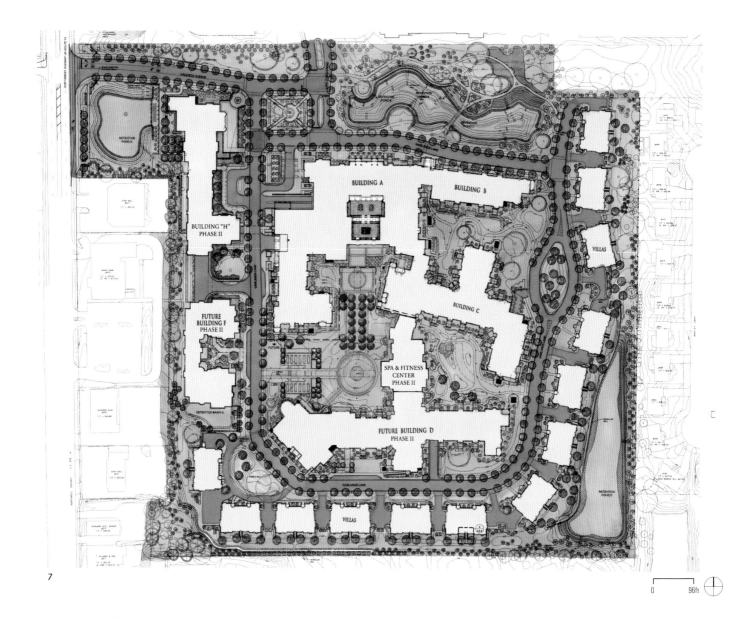

7

BUILDING "H" PHASE II

BUILDING A

BUILDING B

VILLAS

FUTURE BUILDING F PHASE II

BUILDING C

SPA & FITNESS CENTER PHASE II

FUTURE BUILDING D PHASE II

VILLAS

RETENTION POND A

0   96ft

8

CURRENTLY APPROVED ROOF HEIGHT

AB   AC   AD   AE   AF.1   AG.2

TSL FOURTH FLOOR
EL 867.33'

TSL THIRD FLOOR
EL 856.67'

TSL SECOND FLOOR
EL 846.67'

TSL FIRST FLOOR
EL 832.67'

TSL GARAGE
EL 821.67'

GUEST ROOM   CORR   GUEST ROOM

RESIDENCE   MECH   CORR   RESIDENCE

CORR   RESIDENCE

PORCH   LOUNGE   DINING   EGRESS

GARAGE LEVEL

0   15ft

Master Suite No. 1
11'-7" x 15'-3"

Living Room
11'-6" x 19'-2"

Optional
Divider

Master Suite No. 2
11'-7" x 15'-3"

Den
10'-3" x 15'-2"

Fireplace,
Standard

Walk-in
Closet

Walk-in
Closet

Walk-in
Closet

W/D

Walk-in
Closet

Dining Room
11'-6" x 9'-1"

Kitchen
9'-4" x 14'-9"

Master Bath
No. 1

Powder
Room

Foyer

Table
Space

HVAC

Master Bath
No. 2

Seat

9

0   4ft

7   Site plan

8   Building section

9   Independent living unit floor plan

Photography: *Steve Hall/Hedrich–Blessing*

HANDMAKER JEWISH SERVICES FOR THE AGING – RUBIN CAMPUS TUCSON, ARIZONA

Gresham & Beach Architects / Associate architect: Lizard Rock Designs, LLC

Architect's statement

The design team collaborated with the client's financial and marketing consultants and wrote a space program that met current market demand and built in flexibility, to adapt to new demand trends and stricter assisted living regulations. The financing model required that the nursing home continue to generate revenue during construction, so 120,000 square feet of new construction was added to an existing and occupied 7-acre campus.

To preserve its reputation in the community, the client wanted a project that appears woven into its adjacent residential context. Since fundraising was essential to lowering the debt service, the design needed to embed the Jewish community at the center of the new campus. The client anticipated a trend in government regulation that would increasingly force assisted living centers to meet hospital and nursing home standards of construction and fire safety; the design allows for this flexibility.

The client wanted to avoid endless, repetitive corridors with apartments that don't meet the needs of an aging population. The design organizes apartments in residential clusters or 'neighborhoods,' and distills the spaces and functions of each apartment down to an elder-friendly scale.

1

2

Site location	Urban
Site area	6.38 acres/277,725 square feet
Capacity	14 cottages/villas; 90 assisted living units; 32 special care for persons with dementia; 48 skilled care nursing beds
Total project cost	$13 M

3

Major design objectives

Be a good neighbor. Create a plan that belongs to its region and neighborhood that is not isolated in a sea of parking, and that connects residents to their community.

Provide a vibrant central public space, that can be the heart of the community, with activities and destinations that will draw residents out of their apartments and bring out the community.

Make a truly flexible plan, where buildings can be converted at minimal cost to respond to changing types of care demanded over time by the market. Include multifunction public spaces which can host community events or house satellite programs on-site to reduce overheads.

Design residential-scale spaces, neighborhoods within the campus that will give residents a sense of ownership and protection, and will make orientation and wayfinding easier.

Create elder-friendly apartments, scaled to the increasing physical and economic frailty of aging residents.

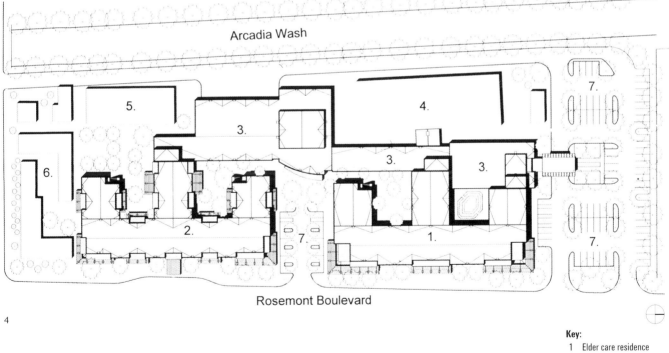

4

1   Street view of project and context

2   Assisted living courtyard

3   Exterior view of dementia care covered porches

4   Site plan

Key:

1   Elder care residence
2   Assisted living residence
3   Commons building
4   Rich nursing pavilion
5   Office/adult day care
6   Besserman apartments
7   Parking

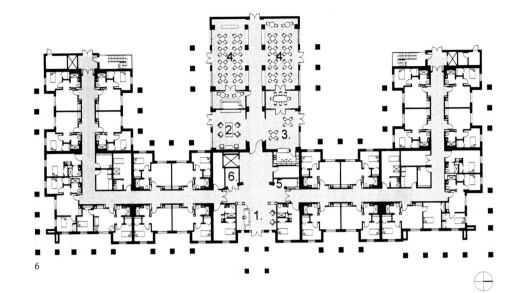

6

5

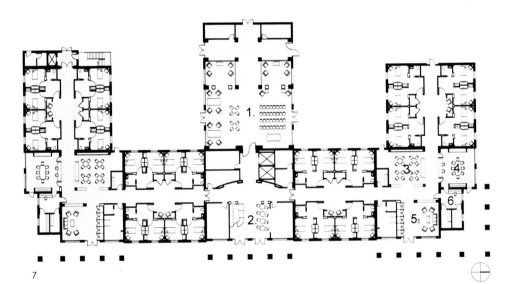

7

5   *Garden window seat*

6   *Assisted living residence floor plan*

7   *Elder care residence floor plan*

8   *Main entrance lobby*

9   *Assisted living dining room*

10   *Typical resident apartment*

Photography: *Liam Frederick*

8

10

9

MARSH'S EDGE

ST. SIMON'S ISLAND, GEORGIA

Cochran, Stephenson & Donkervoet, Inc.

Architect's statement

This new community is located in a part of coastal Georgia that combines great natural beauty with sophisticated cultural resources. St. Simon's Island has managed to avoid over-development, yet enjoys the refined services and conveniences found in urban settings. While the area draws many retirees, the lack of a full-service senior community eventually forced many in this aging population to leave the area.

Marsh's Edge is being designed to meet this need by providing a 325-resident, high-end CCRC. Designed to be built in two phases, the campus includes a 45,000-square-foot commons, apartments that range from 822 to 1,886 square feet, and cottages that range from 2,300 to 2,500 square feet. Higher entrance fees are offset by high site development costs and large building area per resident. Every aspect of the design, therefore, does double duty. The quality demanded by the community is achieved through creative design, rather than high square-foot cost. The site is typical of the island: beautiful, low-lying, with huge live oaks. The highest elevation is well below flood elevation, and it is bisected by a wetland.

1

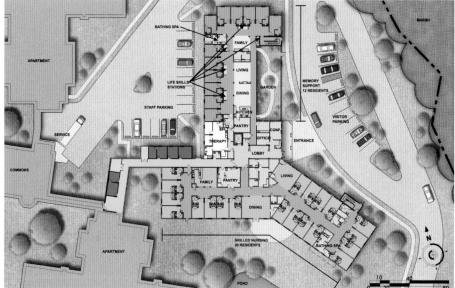

2

3

Site location	Suburban
Site area	36 acres
Capacity	114 apartments; 30 cottages/ villas; 20 assisted living units; 12 special care for persons with dementia; 20 skilled nursing care beds
Total project cost	Not known

1   Rendering of commons
2   Health center first floor plan
3   Health center elevation
4   Commons plan
5   Site plan
6&8   Redfern cottage
7   Hawkins cottage

Major design objectives and responses

Enhance the vitality of residents through design, amenities, and programs

The campus layout is designed to encourage walking, with wellness and social facilities centrally located.

Offer residents the security of knowing that their homes are designed to preserve independence, and that all levels of care are available if needed

Main buildings are connected by air-conditioned routes to prevent summer heat from becoming a barrier to movement.

Provide residents with the ability to live with dignity and to maintain the highest possible level of control over their lives

The buildings evoke the resorts of the area and avoid institutionality. At every level of care, the natural environment is accessible.

Offer residents continued enjoyment of the unique lifestyle and environment of St. Simon's Island

The exterior space of the community is its foremost amenity. Units are large and extensive commons facilities are provided.

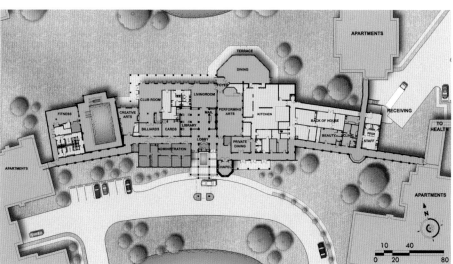

4

6

7

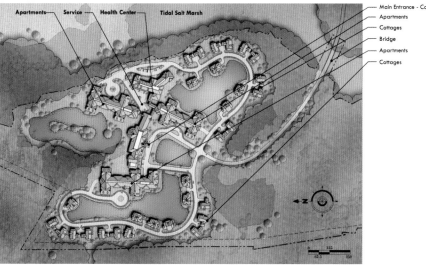

5

8

MASONIC VILLAGE AT SEWICKLEY

SEWICKLEY, PENNSYLVANIA

Perkins Eastman

Architect's statement

Masonic Village at Sewickley is designed to provide a residential setting for the phased development of 228 independent living apartments, 35 independent living cottages, 60 assisted living beds and 128 nursing beds (existing). A wellness center is located centrally and attached to the assisted living building, which includes a children's day care facility, a medical clinic, and a swimming pool. A residents' clubhouse provides dining rooms, common and activity rooms, a country store, and the main multipurpose room and auditorium.

The site design and building placement is intended to evoke the character of a village with the town green as the symbolic and practical center of the community. This is where all of the shared or common buildings are located and where the residents of the cottages, independent living apartments, assisted living residences, visitors, and staff come together.

Site location	Suburban
Site area	50 acres/2,178,009 square feet
Capacity	228 apartments; 35 cottages/ villas; 60 assisted living units; 128 skilled nursing care beds
Total project cost	$70 M

2

Major design objectives and responses

A unique sense of an established community

The planning settled on establishing a large village green in the center of the site upon which all shared fitness and community spaces front. The independent living apartment program was broken down into six buildings of 35–40 units that are all entirely connected to the clubhouse.

A quality of architecture rooted in time

The Village at Sewickley could not replicate a gothic Versailles-inspired architecture and landscape, but the design responds with a solution that is both at home in the brick vernacular of western Pennsylvania, while being distinctive in the interpretation of English and Arts and Crafts architecture. The 'craft' aspect of building (a Masonic trademark) is integrated in the exterior and interior architecture as well as the materials and finishes.

Programs for seniors in the 21st century

There are two dining choices in four differently styled restaurants and wellness/fitness options in a 12,000-square-foot aquatic and exercise center. Intellectual pursuits are met in a library, computer training center, classrooms and large meeting rooms. The site offers walking trails, terraces, and shaded verandas, and it also incorporates a childcare center for intergenerational opportunities and experiences.

3

1&3 *Clubhouse*
2 *Assisted living building*

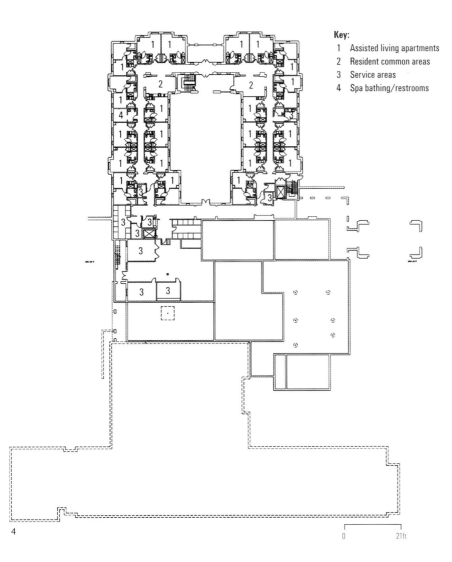

Key:

1. Assisted living apartments
2. Resident common areas
3. Service areas
4. Spa bathing/restrooms

4

0   21ft

5

4   *Assisted living ground floor plan*

5   *Assisted living building main staircase*

6   *Assisted living dining*

7   *Community center lower floor plan*

8   *Independent living floor plans*

9   *Clubhouse dining*

6

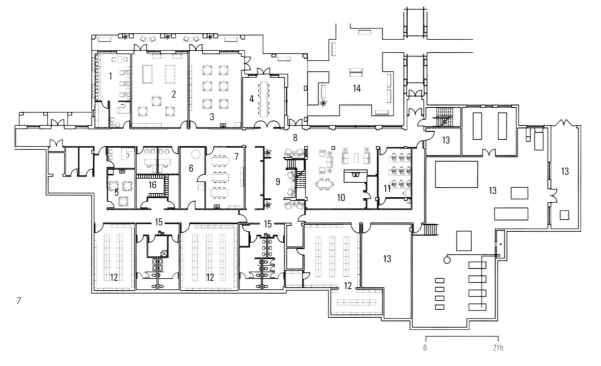

Key:
1 Hair salon
2 Billiards/game room
3 Painting studio
4 Meeting room
5 Staff break room
6 Kiln room
7 Ceramics studio
8 Gallery
9 Stair/hall
10 Library
11 Computer room
12 Storage
13 Service areas
14 Patio
15 Restrooms
16 Locker

0   21ft

7

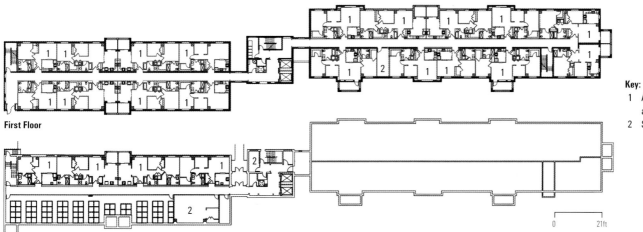

First Floor

Terrace Level

Key:
1 Assisted living
   apartments
2 Service areas

0   21ft

8

9

10

11

12

13

10 *Cultured stone fireplace and custom*
   marble mosaic of Masonic symbol

11 *Clubhouse entry*

12 *Independent living resident apartment*

13 *Library*

Photography: *Massery Photography*

MERCY RIDGE

TIMONIUM, MARYLAND

Cochran, Stephenson & Donkervoet, Inc.

Architect's statement

Developed as a joint venture of two major institutions, the community occupies 32 acres on a rolling suburban site north of Baltimore City. One of the project's most significant design successes is that this large complex of buildings was neatly integrated into a difficult site, creating a living environment that is both attractive and comfortable inside and out, and that provides activity opportunities for both the physically able and the physically challenged. Occupancy of the facility, which includes 259 independent living apartments, a 30-bed assisted living facility, and a large community center, began in July 2001.

The success of the project can be measured by the fact that occupancy reached 90 percent in six months, and two years after the first resident moved in, construction began on Phase II. This will add 149 apartments, 17 assisted living units, a swimming pool, a third dining venue, and a specialized auditorium.

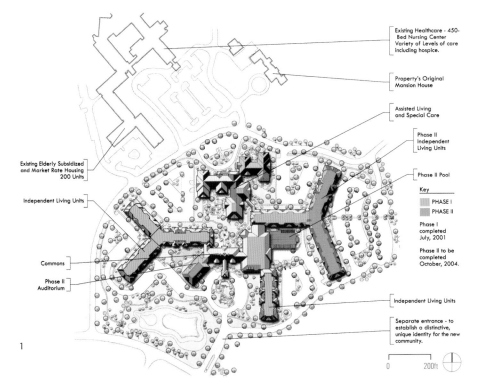

Existing Healthcare - 450-Bed Nursing Center Variety of Levels of care including hospice.

Property's Original Mansion House

Assisted Living and Special Care

Phase II Independent Living Units

Phase II Pool

Key

PHASE I
PHASE II

Phase I completed July, 2001

Phase II to be completed October, 2004.

Existing Elderly Subsidized and Market Rate Housing 200 Units

Independent Living Units

Commons

Phase II Auditorium

Independent Living Units

Separate entrance - to establish a distinctive, unique identity for the new community.

1

0   200ft

2

3

Site location	Suburban
Site area	32.6 acres/1,422,000 square feet
Capacity	259 apartments; 18 assisted living units; 12 special care for persons with dementia
Total project cost	Not known

1   Campus plan
2   Assisted living dining room
3   Main formal dining room
4   Commons, first floor plan
5   Main library
6   Assisted living library

Photography: *Alain Jaramillo (2,6); Alan Gilbert (3,5)*

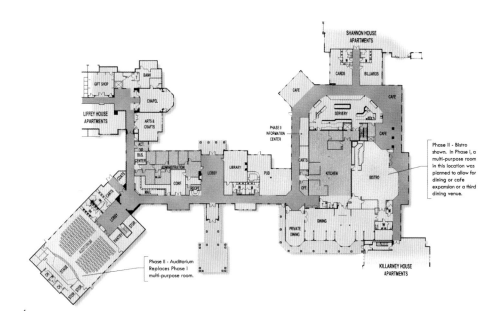

4

5

6

Major design objectives and responses

Provide a wide range of activities for residents

Amenities available include a formal dining room, casual café, fitness center, arts and crafts space, convenience store, bank, beauty/barber shop, wood shop, and a small chapel that features historic stained glass windows. Residents are encouraged to participate in various fitness programs and regular health conferences with a visiting nurse in the Wellness Center. Outdoor amenities include a putting green, bocce court, fountains, and a variety of gardens. An external path system is used for pedestrian circulation and exercise.

Accommodate resident aging-in-place

The interior of the facility is wheelchair accessible throughout and has convenient Amigo® cart parking spaces in the apartment buildings and at central activity spaces. A resident can access the community facilities or visit a friend in any apartment unit or in the assisted living facility without going outside or traversing a single stair. Along the way there are many opportunities for the residents to sit and rest at corridor intersections inside or in pleasant gardens outside.

Each apartment is designed to be fully wheelchair or walker accessible with ample circulation space, large doorways, and grab bars at appropriate locations. The apartments have voice-activated emergency call systems, the portable pendants of which are functional anywhere in the community.

Provide spiritual support

Although not specifically targeted, a high percentage of the residents are Roman Catholic. A small chapel within the facility has become a center of activity for an enthusiastic group of residents who plan daily chapel services. In Phase II, the improved auditorium space will replace the present multipurpose room. Design details of the new space will make it well-suited to larger religious gatherings.

NEWCASTLE PLACE

MEQUON, WISCONSIN

AG Architecture

Architect's statement

The challenge of designing and gaining approval for this $32-million showcase proved to be an invigorating challenge for the entire development team. The approval was difficult because issues concerning density, building size, traffic, and impact on surrounding property values were paramount in the community's mind. In addition, the unique characteristics of the site, including its existing environmental features, as well as patterns of surrounding development, had significant impact on how the building was sited and designed. Finally, a well-crafted public relations effort, featuring intensive community education sessions and strong local senior support, combined with a thoughtful and sensitive design solution, earned municipal approval.

1 Community courtyard
2 Main entry to the site
3 Exterior view of dining room
4 One-story carriage homes
5 Two-story assisted living wings

1

2

3

Site location	Suburban
Site area	50.35 acres/ 2,193,076 square feet
Capacity	81 apartments; 10 cottages/villas; 36 assisted living units; 16 special care for persons with dementia; 47 skilled nursing care beds
Total project cost	$37.76 M

Major design objectives and responses

Use the site's political and physical constraints to inspire the design solution

The density, scale, height, massing, and architectural details of this single project were unprecedented in the community. There were typical concerns about traffic, the effect on surrounding property values, and a general lack of understanding.

Physical constraints included a 13-acre wooded area that divided the site in half, local zoning ordinances that prohibited removal of any major trees, and significant wetlands that were located adjacent to the wooded area as well as the eastern boundaries of the site.

Embrace natural features while effectively managing less desirable aspects

The existing woodlands and wetlands were embraced by locating the larger three-story independent living wings adjacent to them. This allowed most residents to have terrific views from their apartments.

Less desirable views were ignored by turning the large common areas inward toward a different sort of man-made amenity. Because views to the east toward an interstate highway and future on-ramp were less inspired, and the natural views of the woodlands and wetlands were assigned to resident apartments, a community courtyard was created. The main entry/lobby, chapel, library, dining, multipurpose, and various social activities focus on this central exterior space. The change of the seasons can be easily observed while natural light generously flows throughout the entire commons area.

Create a sense that this community is perceived and organized as a village

From the outset, the design team chose to pursue an unconventional and more randomly patterned concept. Site constraints began to further reinforce the village-like solution that was desired by all. Detached carriage homes and two distinct points of public entry into the main building itself also support the concept.

4   5

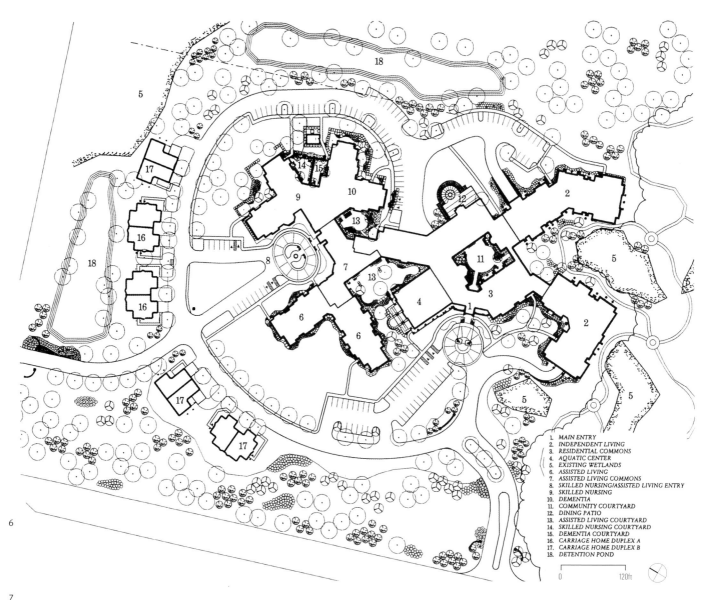

6

0   120ft

7

6　Site plan

7　Pool

8　Fitness center

9　Commons plan

8

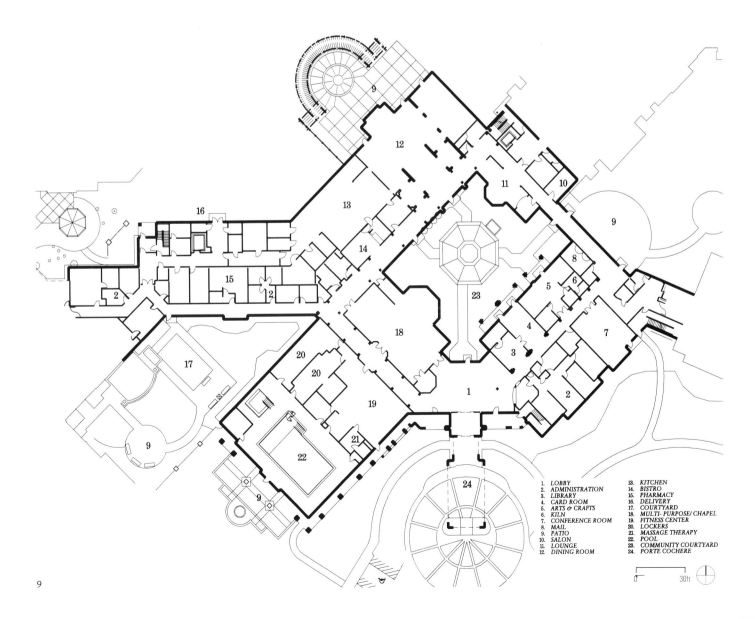

9

1.	LOBBY	13.	KITCHEN
2.	ADMINISTRATION	14.	BISTRO
3.	LIBRARY	15.	PHARMACY
4.	CARD ROOM	16.	DELIVERY
5.	ARTS & CRAFTS	17.	COURTYARD
6.	KILN	18.	MULTI- PURPOSE/ CHAPEL
7.	CONFERENCE ROOM	19.	FITNESS CENTER
8.	MAIL	20.	LOCKERS
9.	PATIO	21.	MASSAGE THERAPY
10.	SALON	22.	POOL
11.	LOUNGE	23.	COMMUNITY COURTYARD
12.	DINING ROOM	24.	PORTE COCHERE

0　　　　　　30ft

10

11

12

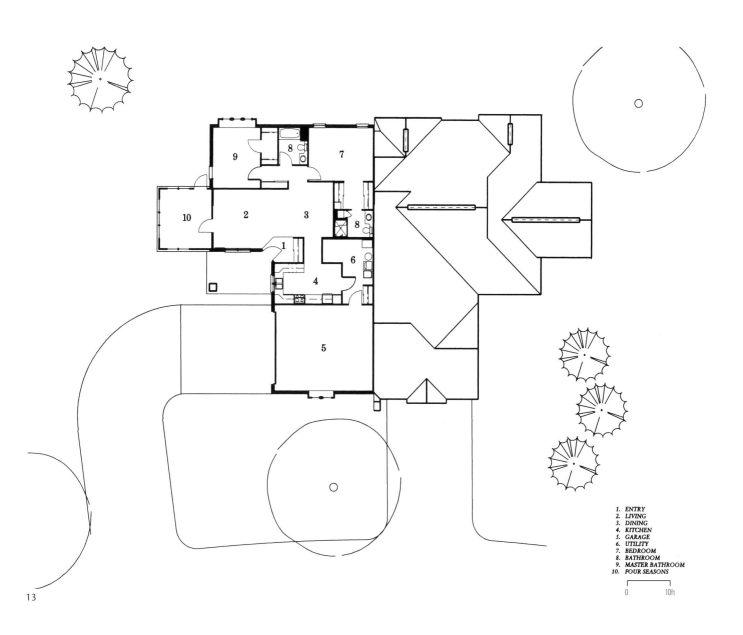

13

1. ENTRY
2. LIVING
3. DINING
4. KITCHEN
5. GARAGE
6. UTILITY
7. BEDROOM
8. BATHROOM
9. MASTER BATHROOM
10. FOUR SEASONS

0   10ft

14

10 Main lobby

11 Dining room

12 Library and game room areas

13 Carriage home B floor plan

14 Grand hallway

Photography: *John J. Korom Photography*

Piper Shores

Scarborough, Maine

EGA, P.C.

Architect's statement

The site is an unusual oceanfront property offering spectacular views, the same that inspired painter Winslow Homer. The design challenge was how to respond to the opportunities and constraints offered by this beautiful but ocean oriented site. Responding to these issues, the masterplan was developed with the major independent living commanding the primary views. Flanking this common area on either side are the independent living apartments, arranged so that the majority of apartments have water views. Assisted living and long term care utilize the same service component, centrally located but focused away from the ocean, as the independent living commons. The architecture is a contemporary interpretation of historic resort hotels which were prevalent in New England's history.

Site location	Suburban
Site area	138 acres
Capacity	212 apartments;
	40 cottages/villas
Total project cost	$26.6 M

1

2

3

4

Major design objectives and responses

Capitalize on the opportunities offered by the site

Since the budget was modest, this had to be accomplished with inexpensive solutions. The design consists primarily of a double-loaded, three-story apartment stack. By careful placement and orientation, the scheme allows 70 percent of the independent living apartments to have ocean views. Exterior walls are chamfered to allow views diagonal to the coast and into courtyards rather than into other apartments. Additionally, the apartment wings are stepped one from another to take advantage, whenever possible, of multiple exposures for all the apartments. This helps to present a building that appears to be smaller in scale. Internally, this design feature provides a corridor system that allows daylight in numerous areas, providing a more enriching walk to the commons as well as frequent wayfinding cues. Internal lounges are provided along corridors to allow interest and resting areas. To take advantage of the spectacular views the dining rooms and kitchen were placed on the top floor. Instead of one large dining room, the design incorporates five smaller rooms, providing better sound qualities and more intimate scale.

1   *Exterior view toward entry*
2&3   *Exterior*
4   *Largest unit floor plan*

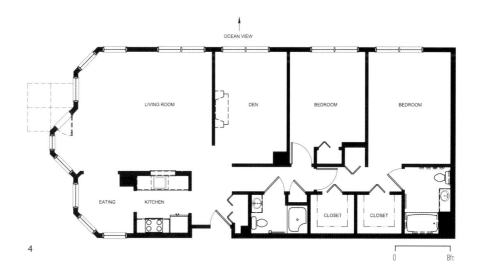

OCEAN VIEW

LIVING ROOM   DEN   BEDROOM   BEDROOM

EATING   KITCHEN   CLOSET   CLOSET

0   8ft

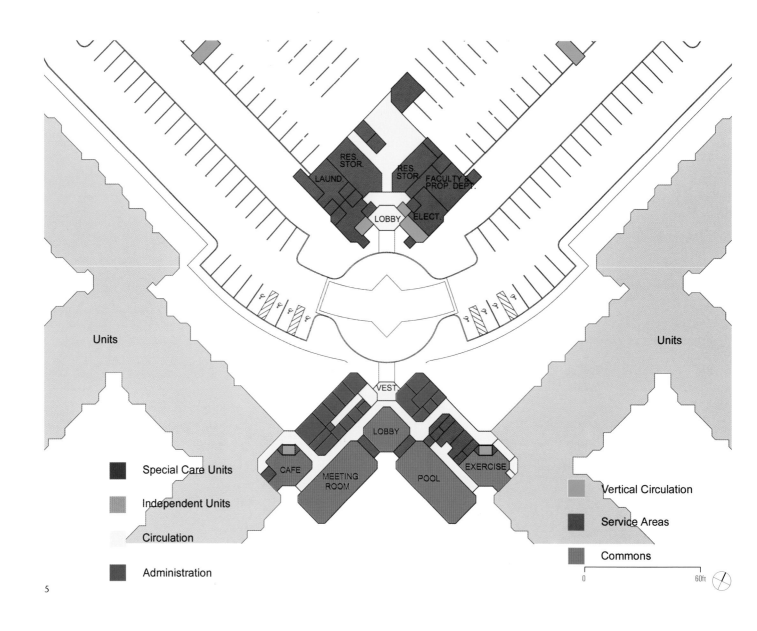

RES.
STOR.

RES.
STOR.

LAUND

FACULTY &
PROP. DEPT.

ELECT.

LOBBY

Units

Units

VEST.

LOBBY

CAFE

MEETING
ROOM

POOL

EXERCISE

■ Special Care Units

■ Independent Units

☐ Circulation

■ Administration

■ Vertical Circulation

■ Service Areas

■ Commons

0   60ft

5

6

7

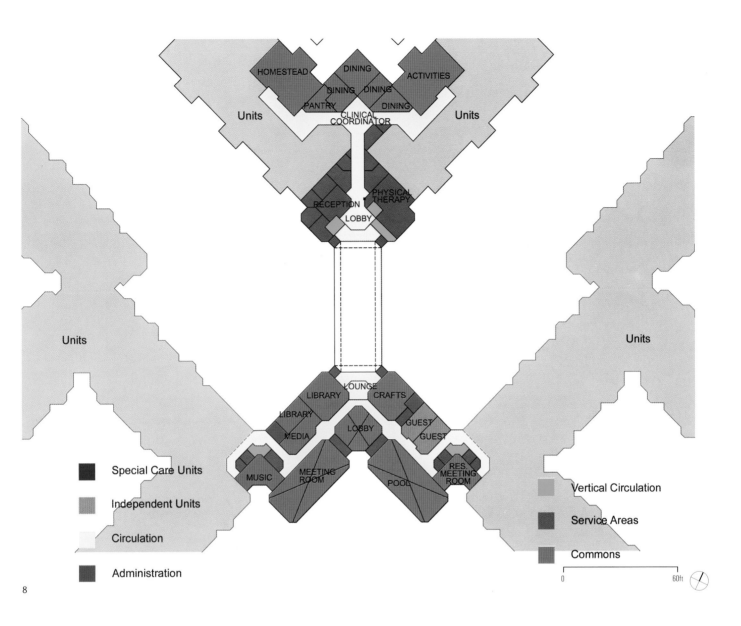

Special Care Units

Independent Units

Circulation

Administration

Vertical Circulation

Service Areas

Commons

0   60ft

8

9

10

5 Ground floor commons plan
6 Main dining room
7 Library
8 Second floor commons plan
9 Meeting room
10 Pool

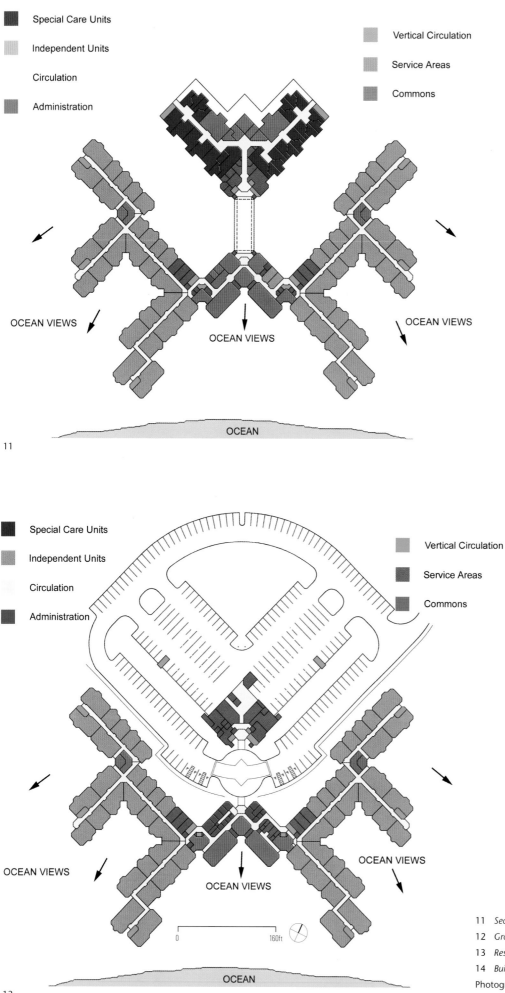

Legend (top plan)

- Special Care Units
- Independent Units
- Circulation
- Administration
- Vertical Circulation
- Service Areas
- Commons

OCEAN VIEWS

OCEAN VIEWS

OCEAN VIEWS

OCEAN VIEWS

OCEAN

11

Legend (bottom plan)

- Special Care Units
- Independent Units
- Circulation
- Administration
- Vertical Circulation
- Service Areas
- Commons

OCEAN VIEWS

OCEAN VIEWS

OCEAN VIEWS

OCEAN VIEWS

0   160ft

OCEAN

12

13

11   *Second floor plan*
12   *Ground floor plan*
13   *Resident apartment*
14   *Building section*
Photography: *Assassi Productions*

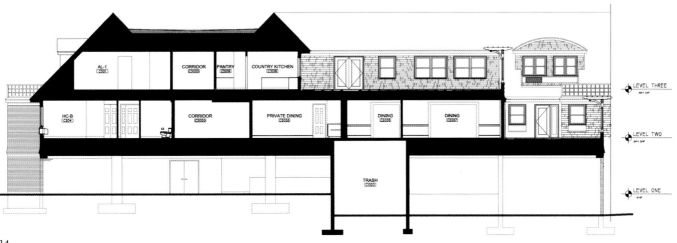

14

Westminster–Canterbury on Chesapeake Bay Virginia Beach, Virginia

SFCS Inc.

Architect's statement

Location and incredible views are just two of the reasons why seniors enjoy life at this CCRC. This lifecare community was recently expanded and renovated to enhance the lives of existing and future boomer residents. The community's goal is to stay focused on resident services and wellness through the management approach and facility design. A new 14-story residential tower (west) with a serpentine shape maximizes views from the 164 new market-rate apartments. Large balconies expand the already spacious living apartments. The previous community had over 300 independent living apartments, 53 assisted living units and 72 nursing care beds on the 12-acre, bay-front site. After the renovation, the existing 15-story tower (east) offers two floors of enhanced services (assisted living) for a total of 56 units. Conversions, combinations, and apartment upgrades are ongoing in the east tower, which has the capacity of 300 apartments.

1   Main entrance with porte-cochere
2   West tower
3   Serpentine design provides everyone with bay views
4   Under construction

1

Site location	Suburban
Site area	12.78 acres
Capacity	164 apartments; 91 assisted living units; 14 special care for persons with dementia; 72 skilled nursing care beds
Total project cost	$60.5 M

2

3

4

Major design objectives and responses

Unify the community, add amenities to improve quality of life for existing residents, and attract new residents

The west tower adds a ground floor mainstreet, which includes a new 300-person multipurpose room, chapel, barber/beauty, country store, bank, library, living room, a second pool, exercise facility, and juice bar. The ground floor connects the towers to the healthcare building, unifying the community. A new main entrance and concierge area was created. New porte-cocheres with a wave design are featured at the new main entrance and the previous healthcare entrance.

Add parking to the site

A five-story, 435-space parking garage was added.

Create additional outdoor spaces

A wrap-around patio extends along the main dining room and mainstreet living area, giving easy access to the outside. Residents can enjoy croquet, boche ball, one of four garden areas, or a stroll on the beach. A meditation garden, a wellness garden, and planter-gardens were also added to the site.

Offer additional levels of assisted living care, improve the healthcare environment, and increase staff efficiency

The previous clinic was renovated to become a new assisted living memorycare household. The remainder of the healthcare center was renovated, increasing the number of private rooms, eliminating large nursing desks, decentralizing services, adding sun porches and upgrading furnishings. The clinic was relocated and redesigned to serve residents and seniors from the community by offering expanded services such as dentistry, podiatry, and dermatology.

Design a quality building with unique architectural elements that would overcome any zoning questions

Models of the design were presented to the city and neighborhood groups to depict how their views would be impacted. These extensive computer-aided models convinced zoning officials that the impact of shadows, sight lines, and noise on the neighbors would be minimal.

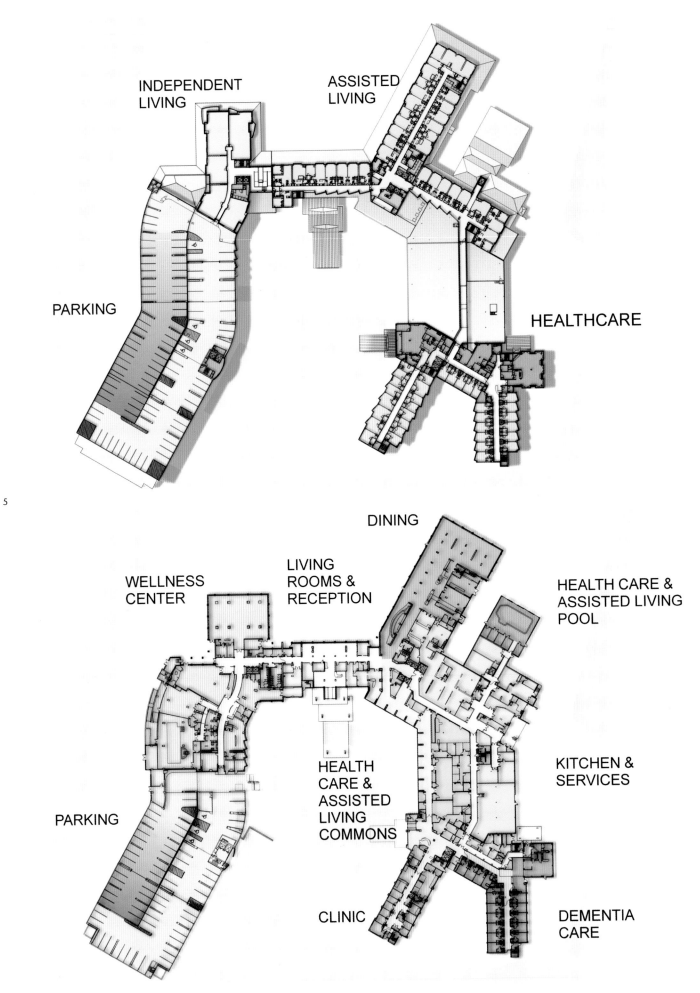

INDEPENDENT
LIVING

ASSISTED
LIVING

PARKING

HEALTHCARE

5

DINING

WELLNESS
CENTER

LIVING
ROOMS &
RECEPTION

HEALTH CARE &
ASSISTED LIVING
POOL

HEALTH
CARE &
ASSISTED
LIVING
COMMONS

KITCHEN &
SERVICES

PARKING

CLINIC

DEMENTIA
CARE

6

7

8

9

5   First and second floor plan
6   Ground floor plan
7&8 Activity area
9   Main dining room
10   Lap pool and hot tub

10

11

12

13

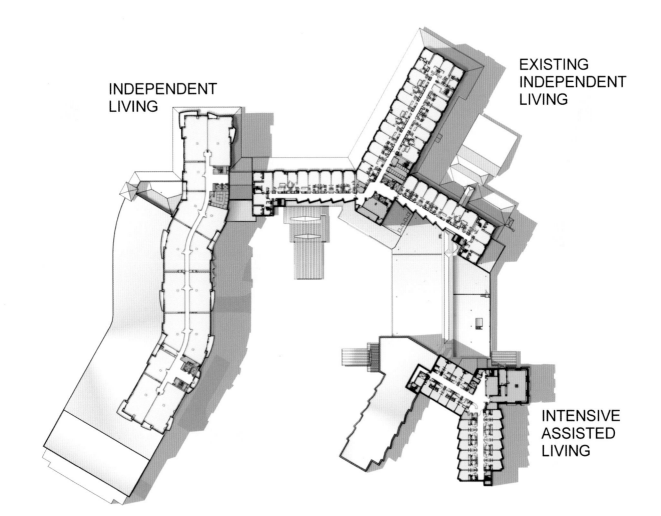

INDEPENDENT
LIVING

EXISTING
INDEPENDENT
LIVING

INTENSIVE
ASSISTED
LIVING

14

15

11 Community living room
12 Chapel with wave ceiling
13 West tower apartment
14 Typical floor plan
15 Bay view room
Photography: *Tim Schoon Photography*

WESTMINSTER-CANTERBURY, INC.

LYNCHBURG, VIRGINIA
SFCS Inc.

Architect's statement

The vision was to integrate significant new program features into an existing community that supported existing operations, and enhanced not only the architecture, but the quality of the environment for residents. This was accomplished with a cost-effective solution that allowed the owner to maintain financial goals and feasibility.

A primary challenge was to minimize disruption during the expansion process, yet every level of care was affected and almost every building was impacted. This was especially complex in the social spaces and many of the resident commons spaces. Having designed the original campus and the previous assisted living addition, an in-depth understanding of the community supported the team approach that included the owner, staff, design team, and contractor to minimize disruptions to the lives of the people who lived and worked there.

1

2

3

4

Site location	Suburban
Site area	4 acres
Capacity	56 apartments; 14 special care for persons with dementia
Total project cost	$20.1 M

1   *Aerial view of campus depicting expansion*

2&3 *Expansion of community center spaces and courtyard 1*

4   *Memory care courtyard*

5&6 *New apartment building showcases balconies*

7   *Wellness facility*

5

6

7

Major design objectives and responses

Design a new wellness center with expanded clinic spaces and an indoor pool and fitness area that is easily accessible to all levels of care

A modern facility was designed in the hub of activity on the campus located near the healthcare, assisted living and independent living residents. Employees also enjoy a new staff break area, lockers, and classroom spaces.

Design a new assisted living memory care unit

A new 14-bed residential model household with an atrium area connected the expansion to the existing social model AL building, provides easy staff access throughout. The new memory care unit has a secure courtyard, sunroom, living room, activity/kitchen/dining, and open staff spaces.

Design new and expanded community center spaces

New and improved dining facilities added a café for staff and residents. Optional buffet-style or wait service is available in two distinct dining venues within the renovated main dining room. The design provides for sectional areas, giving residents more privacy during meal times.

Create new and expanded resident common spaces

The main lobby and community center was extended to include a larger lobby and concierge space as well as marketing offices. The administrative office suite was relocated to be more accessible. The glass walls bring natural light into the new art studio, arts and craft space, and lounge and billiard room. Expanded multipurpose areas now access a roof-top patio affording residents with views of the pastoral countryside. The library was also relocated to ease resident use.

Design a new independent living apartment building to assist in financing the other campus expansions, as well as meet the current and future market demands

A new five-story, 56-unit apartment building was designed adjacent to the newly expanded community center. The apartments range from 700 to 1,475 square feet and feature large balconies/patios, modern amenities, and a variety of unit styles.

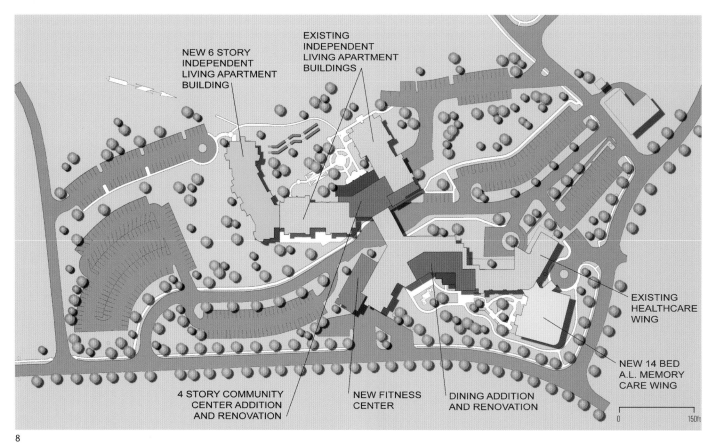

NEW 6 STORY
INDEPENDENT
LIVING APARTMENT
BUILDING

EXISTING
INDEPENDENT
LIVING APARTMENT
BUILDINGS

EXISTING
HEALTHCARE
WING

NEW 14 BED
A.L. MEMORY
CARE WING

4 STORY COMMUNITY
CENTER ADDITION
AND RENOVATION

NEW FITNESS
CENTER

DINING ADDITION
AND RENOVATION

0   150ft

8

9

10

11

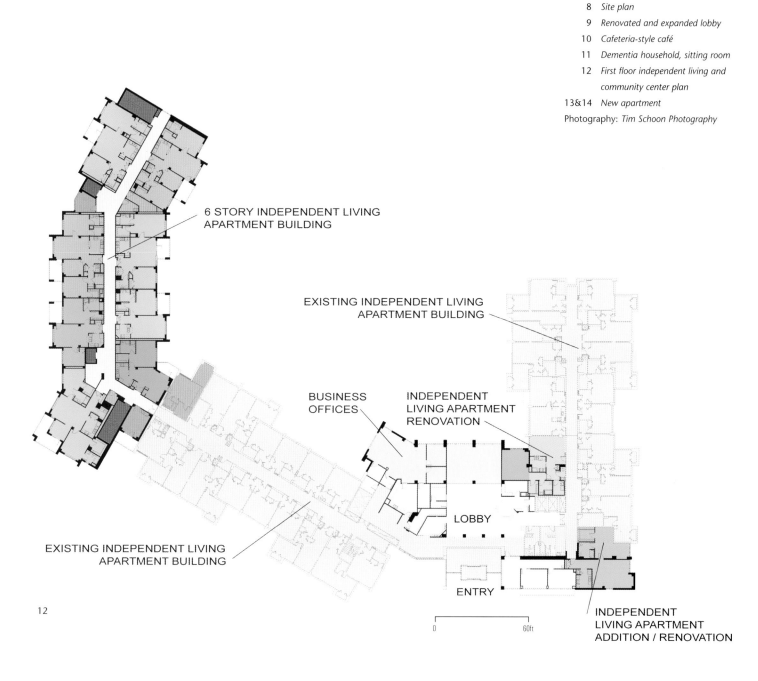

6 STORY INDEPENDENT LIVING
APARTMENT BUILDING

EXISTING INDEPENDENT LIVING
APARTMENT BUILDING

BUSINESS
OFFICES

INDEPENDENT
LIVING APARTMENT
RENOVATION

EXISTING INDEPENDENT LIVING
APARTMENT BUILDING

LOBBY

ENTRY

INDEPENDENT
LIVING APARTMENT
ADDITION / RENOVATION

12

0   60ft

13

14

WILLIAMSBURG LANDING, EDGEWOOD EXPANSION WILLIAMSBURG, VIRGINIA

Cochran, Stephenson & Donkervoet, Inc.

Architect's statement

Williamsburg Landing is a 20-year-old, existing CCRC sited on 133 beautifully landscaped acres neighboring Colonial Williamsburg, Virginia. The community currently consists of two distinct cottage neighborhoods, two manor-style apartment buildings, and a central community building, as well as an assisted living and skilled nursing component.

To respond to increasing competition and the needs of a changing marketplace, Williamsburg Landing has initiated a three-phase expansion that includes the construction of an additional neighborhood of 32 cottages and 31 manor-style apartment units. The expansion also includes a new 20,000-square-foot wellness and fitness spa with a full aquatics program. The entire new neighborhood is designed using the 'New Urbanism' approach to planning and a traditional architectural style reminiscent of Colonial Williamsburg.

1

Site location	Suburban
Site area	25.48 acres/1,109,909 square feet
Capacity	31 apartments; 32 cottages/villas
Total project cost	Not known

2

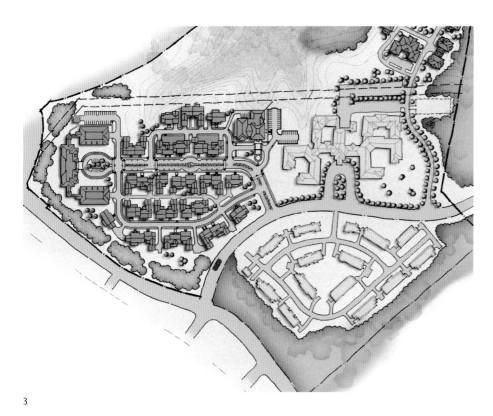

3

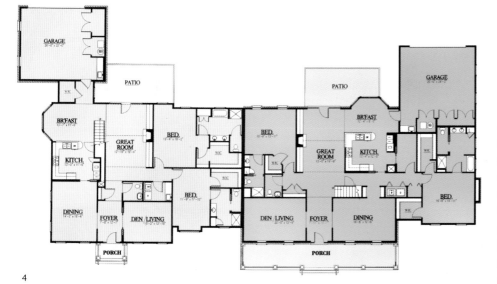

4

5

Major design objectives and responses

Create a state-of-the-art, holistic wellness program and reinforce it through enhanced usage of the site's natural resources
Design a vibrant wellness facility for physical exercise, social interaction, emotional support, and intellectual and creative fulfillment.

Offset the cost of development and operations of the new Wellness Center by optimizing income-producing living units on the remaining undeveloped land on site
Design larger living units with diversity of size, type, amenities, and features, all with a contemporary interior lifestyle in mind, yet with architectural design style and site planning clearly reminiscent of Colonial Williamsburg.

Attract the new generation of seniors and reinforce the desirability of this destination community by providing:
- easy access from adjacent health center
- direct connection to new walking pathways through adjoining woodlands and new landscaped boulevard
- welcoming gateway to the new neighborhood
- open outdoor convocation space at the main entrance

Add a new distinctive neighborhood in the established tradition of this community and establish a vibrant secondary hub to attract resident involvement in wellness site-wide
Utilize traditional neighborhood development concepts to plan the new neighborhood with higher density of living units, distinctive architecture, richly appointed infrastructure, and emphasis on pedestrian walkways and community interactions.

1 *Manor house apartments*
2 *Wellness center*
3 *Site master plan*
4 *Duplex cottage plan*
5 *Street perspective*

DESIGN FOR

ASSISTED LIVING FACILITY

FACILITY

GING REVIEW

Cuthbertson Village at Aldersgate
Charlotte, North Carolina

FreemanWhite, Inc

Citation · *The attention paid to the organization and layering of communities in this nursing residence addition yielded a design that responds to the individual both outside and inside. The plan creatively overcomes regulatory restrictions, while recognizing staffing needs and assisting in resident orientation. The central community space provides an appealing, naturally lit gathering place for residents.*

Architect's statement

Cuthbertson Village incorporates the 'Eden Alternative™' philosophy and Main Street concepts into a holistic environment for seniors with memory impairment that promotes positive interaction among residents, staff, families, and the community. The 45-bed village is divided into three households, each home to 15 residents occupying private rooms and sharing a residential-scale living room, dining room, country kitchen, family room and back porch. Each household connects to outdoor courtyards and to the central town square, which includes a general store, cinema, pet store, café, and garden shop surrounding a central garden with walking path, goldfish pond, stage and aviary. Each area has expanded life skill stations where residents can participate in or observe the activities, providing what the staff calls 'purposeful pathways' throughout the village. From morning until bedtime, the residents are free to move throughout all areas of their household and village.

1

2

3

Site location	Suburban
Site area	3.4 acres/148,104 square feet
Capacity	45 special care for persons with dementia
Total project cost	$4 M

Major design objectives and responses

Create a holistic living environment for seniors with memory impairment to enhance quality of life through their remaining years

Using the Eden Alternative™ as the project's guiding philosophy, the residents have an independent and caring environment, allowing them to have broad, positive interaction with their surroundings. Fundamentally, the whole village creates a strong visual, olfactory, and touch-connected experience.

Create an interactive community for residents, their families, staff, children, animals and the larger community

The village and households are filled with dogs, cats, birds, fish, and plants to allow residents to continue to have caring and purposeful experiences throughout their day. Planned activities bring different people in and family members and children visit regularly, providing the village with an age diversity that is reminiscent of the communities they grew up in.

Create a synergistic environment where residents are connected to the rhythms of nature and the seasons of the year

This community allows easy access to the outside from multiple locations, through French doors with sidelights that bring the outside in, and cue the residents to enjoy and experience the garden areas. The skylight in the town square and the large windows throughout the households allow a connection with the normal rhythms of the day and seasons, while the porches and gardens let them enjoy nature and the changing weather.

Create stimulating wayfinding throughout the village to reduce agitation and unfocused wandering

Each household has a distinctly different entry experience, from a brownstone stoop, to a colonial front porch all designed to strongly differentiate the sense of entry between them. Bright colorful signage at eye level is located at the activity centers.

4

5

6

1   Courtyard with swing
2   Town square with skylight
3   'Clip and Curl' beauty shop
4   Public entrance
5   Courtyard dining porch
6   Inner courtyard entry

7

8

7   Potting shed and garden shop

8   Soda fountain shop

9   Household country kitchen

10 Building plan

11 Resident room

12 Household living room

13 Resident spa

Photography: *Tim Mueller (4);*

Tim Buchman (1–3,5–9,11–13)

9

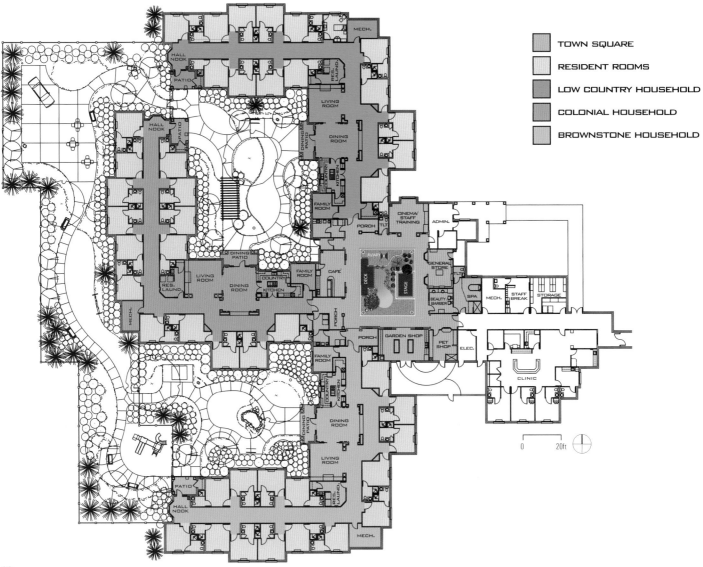

10

TOWN SQUARE

RESIDENT ROOMS

LOW COUNTRY HOUSEHOLD

COLONIAL HOUSEHOLD

BROWNSTONE HOUSEHOLD

11

12

13

This assisted living facility for the memory impaired combines creative use of community spaces with a recognition of the way in which local architecture can provide visual uniqueness without 'faddishness' to help orient residents. In particular, the organization of the residences with clear delineation between them and the 'main street' can help guide residents, as well as their visitors.

THE VILLAGE AT WAVENY CARE CENTER   NEW CANAAN, CONNECTICUT

Reese, Lower, Patrick & Scott, Ltd.

Architect's statement

The solution to the dementia program was to create an area where residents live in smaller neighborhoods, each with its own family room, country kitchen and dining room, to instill a private, comfortable domestic setting. Residents sleep, wake, bathe, and eat in their passive neighborhoods prior to entering the second part of the solution: an adult day program area. Here, 53 residents, along with 30 to 40 daily seniors with dementia, converge into an active program area titled 'mainstreet.' Reminiscent of the local, old-fashioned downtown, mainstreet recaptures many of its positive qualities of scale, proportion, style, and sense of community. Opposing one- and two-story brick and clapboard building façades create a skylit street-housing program space including a beauty/barber shop, bakery, ice cream parlor, general store, and dining piazza. Mainstreet fulfills the active portion of a resident's day, promotes freedom and exploration, offers a seamless connection to the outdoors, and encourages socialization, all in a recognizable, bright and comfortable environment.

1

2

Site location	Small town
Site area	11.7 acres/510,850 square feet
Capacity	53 special care for persons with dementia
Total project cost	$12.1 M

1   Adult daycare home base
2   Mainstreet exterior
3   View down mainstreet
4   Overall floor plan
5   Mainstreet
6   Dining area

3

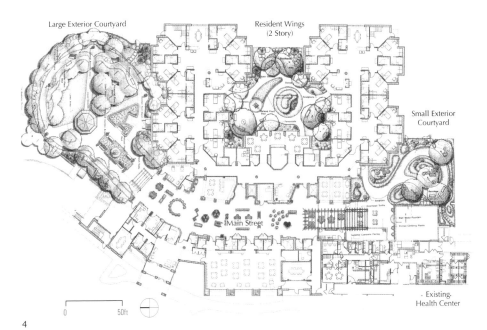

Large Exterior Courtyard

Resident Wings
(2 Story)

Small Exterior
Courtyard

Main Street

0   50ft

Existing
Health Center

4

5

6

Major design objectives and responses

Create an environment that defines active versus passive, or public versus private settings

Small, private neighborhoods of 13 rooms provide the passive or private settings. Rooms are equipped with their own bath and shower to provide a dignified and domestic bathing experience.

Mainstreet captures the charm of downtown New Canaan and becomes the active or public setting, designed to stimulate the senses while triggering distant memories.

Create a homelike environment in the residential wings

Neighborhoods are organized to avoid any sense of corridors. Lighting is indirect through ceiling coves to provide a warm and inviting setting. An open country kitchen that doubles as a staff desk, along with a dining room setting and adjacent family room with a fireplace, further define home. Rooms are private with a large, built-in dresser and wardrobe cabinet facing the corridor, allowing personalization of the area.

Create a 'downtown' to promote a sense of freedom, wandering, and socializing

A 28-foot-wide by 150-foot-long street is defined by opposing one- and two-story building façades. Each façade is a collection of smaller building fronts, some clad in brick and others in clapboard siding of varying colors. Storefront windows, flower boxes, awnings, and a clock tower lend authenticity to the streetscape. A beauty/barber shop, ice cream parlor, bakery, general store, and dining piazza occur through the façades. Carpet resembles cobblestone, and cast street lights, potted trees, and street benches add the finishing touches.

Provide an adult daycare setting for local residents with memory loss

A large, subdivided, multifunctional room or home base is provided adjacent to the main lobby for adult daycare residents. Each of the subdivided areas has a distinctly detailed entrance accessing mainstreet where the residents commingle and participate in the daily activities and programs of the residents living at the facility.

7

8

9

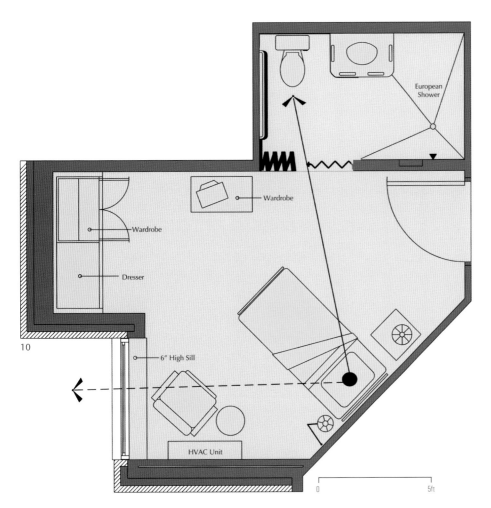

10

Wardrobe

Wardrobe

Dresser

6" High Sill

HVAC Unit

European Shower

0   5ft

7   *Resident room*
8   *Country kitchen*
9   *Bathroom*
10   *Typical resident room floor plan*
11   *Dining area with view to private courtyard*
Photography: *Larry Lefever Photography*

11

This reuse of a historic school building creatively maintains a residential scale. Maintaining the integrity of the building and site while adapting the school's spaces and providing for accessibility gives this assisted living facility both continuity and diversity.

BRIGHAM HOUSE

WATERTOWN, MASSACHUSETTS

The Architectural Team, Inc.

Architect's statement

Built in 1911, this 60,000-square-foot landmark building underwent complete interior and exterior restoration in accordance with the National Park Service's historic preservation guidelines. Since the building originally served as a high school, existing spaces such as the former auditorium were used to locate common areas, including the dining room and lounge. The existing main corridors were retained as circulation paths. This criterion was intended to take advantage of the existing great architectural character and detail present throughout the historic building. The program includes 60 residential studio units, administrative space, and common areas, including living and dining rooms, a bistro, library, and a beauty/barber shop.

General accessibility and circulation patterns presented a challenge, due to the complex system of levels of the original basement and first floor. Existing heavy masonry construction also imposed important structural constraints on the architect's desire of opening and interconnecting the layout as much as possible.

2

1

3

Site location	Suburban
Site area	1.25 acres/54,813 square feet
Capacity	60 assisted living units
Total project cost	$7.5 M

1 New handicapped-accessible
  main entrance
2 Northern façade
3 Southern façade
4 Detail of new main entrance
  and sunken patio
5 Rear façade and garden area

4

5

Major design objectives and responses

Accommodate an assisted living program to serve seniors in an existing high school building that had multiple level changes

The architect took advantage of some of the existing spaces on the lower floors and converted them into common areas. The multiple level changes on the lower floors were resolved by the addition of three elevators and a wheelchair ramp. Common spaces were placed on the lower levels, and the majority of the resident rooms were located on the upper levels of the building.

Preserve and restore important historical details of the original design and include them into the general design of the project

Under guidance of the National Park Service's historic preservation guidelines, the building's façade was restored to its original grand state. Damaged and missing limestone pieces were repaired, windows were completely refurbished with new glass and glazing, and new pulleys and weights were installed. Doors were replaced with custom-designed cherry doors that matched the originals and the new spaces were blended with the old walls and details.

Create a handicapped-accessible main entrance

The original entrances at the front of the building were only accessible by staircases. The main entrance was transferred to the side of the building, where an existing doorway was closer to the ground level. A sunken patio was created, along with a new handicapped-accessible ramp. The original entrance porticos were retained to connect the living areas with the front yard.

Design a coherent circulation system

The original building levels impeded circulation flow, and it was not coherent for the assisted living program. The design interconnected common areas with carefully placed ramps and stairs that did not compromise the historical character. The building was also vertically interconnected at two different locations to create easier access for physically impaired residents.

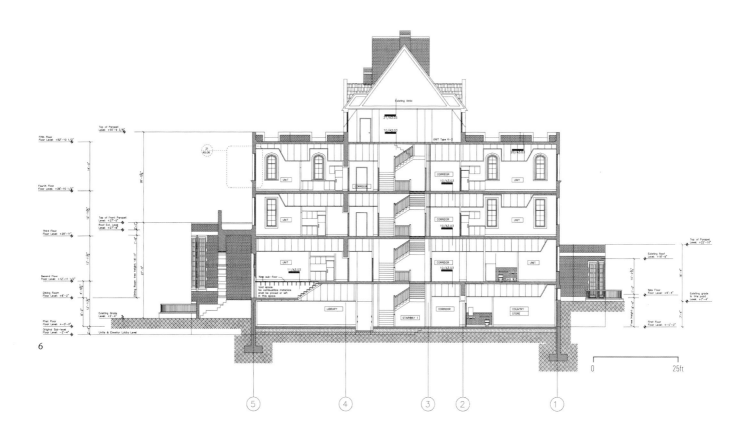

6

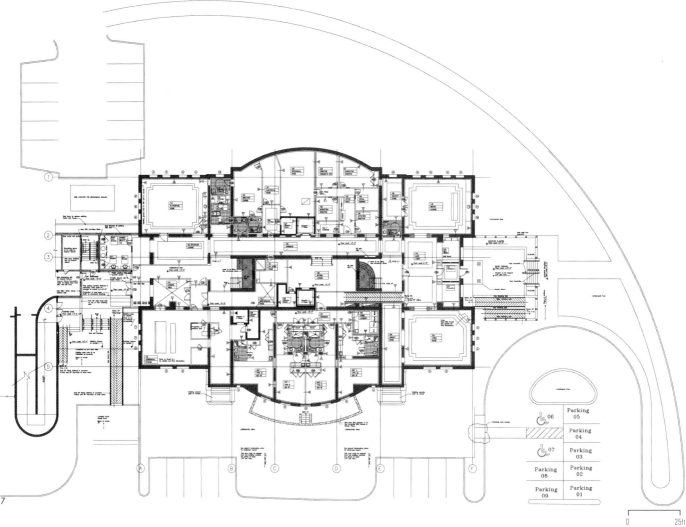

7

♿ 06	Parking 05
	Parking 04
♿ 07	Parking 03
Parking 08	Parking 02
Parking 09	Parking 01

0   25ft

8

9

6   Section

7   Ground floor plan

8   Dining room with view of lounge

9   Living room

Photography: *Bruce T. Martin (1–5);*

David A. Snow (8,9)

HUNTERBROOK RIDGE AND THE SEABURY AT FIELDHOME YORKTOWN HEIGHTS, NEW YORK

Perkins Eastman

Architect's statement

This new facility was planned on a rural campus with an existing 200-bed skilled nursing facility and an outmoded 40-bed assisted living facility with cell-like rooms and common toilet rooms. The new building provides an activity and service focus for the entire campus and has allowed the offering of a true continuum of care. The former building, a historic landmark, is now used as additional space for independent living resident activities as well as meeting space for community organizations.

The dementia care area consists of two houses with sub-clusters of 10 residents. Each house has its own dining, country kitchen and living room, and is designed with a hierarchy of spaces from public to private. Each house also has its own private, secure outdoor courtyard. The two houses share a great room, activity spaces, and a large wandering garden.

1 *Main entrance with covered drop-off*
2 *Assisted living porch off activity room/lounge*
3 *Alzheimer's/dementia care*
4 *Independent living cottage*
5 *Site plan*

1

Site location	Rural
Site area	67 acres/2,919,000 square feet
Capacity	64 units; 40 assisted living units
Total project cost	$18.62 M

2

3

Major design objectives

- Provide a continuum of care
- Create a residential architectural vocabulary that reflects the best qualities of a rural setting with historic structures
- Promote a residential interior with a distinct character, reflecting the familiar tastes of residents of the region
- Maintain small-scale settings
- Create an affordable solution to enable residents in the surrounding area to remain near their friends and lifelong communities

5

4

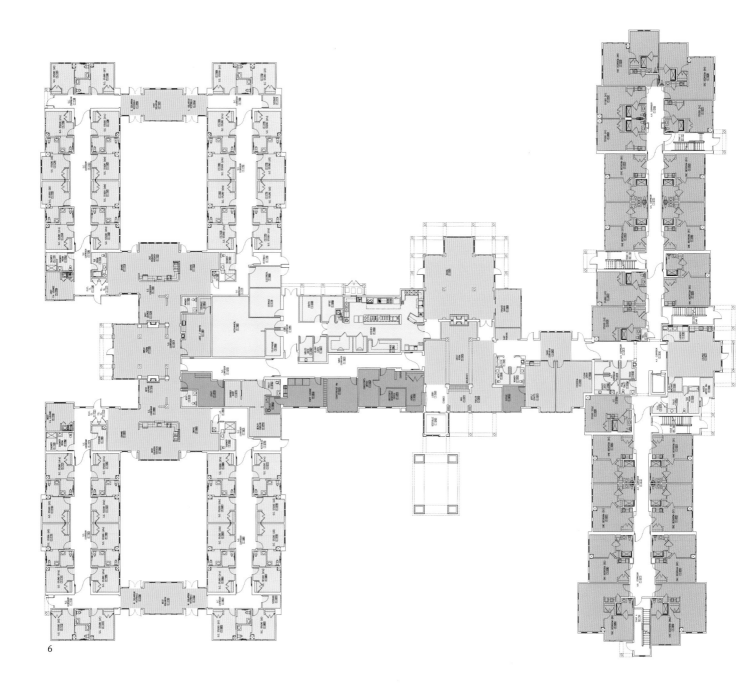

6

6   Assisted living floor plan

7   Country kitchen and dining
     area in dementia care house

8   Main dining room

9   Gathering lounge

7

8

9

10

11

10   Activity room/lounge

11   Cottage living room

12&13   Independent living cottage floor plans

14   Resident apartment

Photography: Chuck Choi

COVERED PORCH
11'-11"x7'-7"

MASTER BEDROOM
14'-0"X12'-0"

BATH
7'-0"x9'-2"

STOR

W.I.C.

LIVING/DINING ROOM
24'-3"X13'-3"

DEN
10'-0"x11'-0"

MECH

GARAGE
11'-0"x22'-0"

KITCHEN
11'-10"x9'-4"

BATH
10'-0"x7'-0"

BKFST AREA
6'-8"X6'-5

12

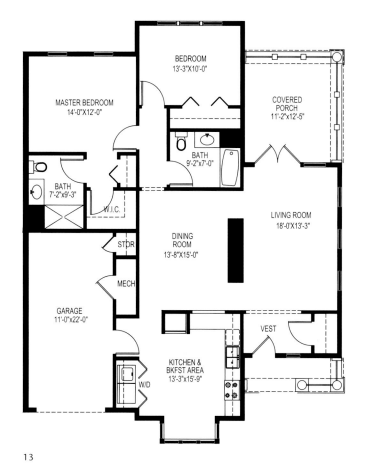

BEDROOM
13'-3"X10'-0"

MASTER BEDROOM
14'-0"X12'-0"

COVERED PORCH
11'-2"x12'-5"

BATH
9'-2"x7'-0"

BATH
7'-2"x9'-3"

W.I.C.

LIVING ROOM
18'-0"X13'-3"

STOR

DINING ROOM
13'-8"X15'-0"

MECH

GARAGE
11'-0"x22'-0"

VEST

KITCHEN & BKFST AREA
13'-3"x15'-9"

W/D

13

14

Keystone Community

FARIBAULT, MINNESOTA

Nelson•Tremain Partnership

Architect's statement

When the elementary school was turned into a community center, the old playground, across from the clinic, was a natural location for a new housing project. With the support of local town government and access to the HUD 232 assisted living loan program, the need for assisted living apartments for frail seniors, as well as for those requiring special cognitive programming, could be met.

Perched above the main road into town, the building presents a familiar image, using understated residential forms and materials. A quiet entry court around the corner allows direct access to both the main entrance and memory care household.

A variety of activity and dining spaces are dispersed throughout the main floor, creating an active central hub for the 42 assisted living apartments. The Creamery and Woolen Room provide imagery and products associated with surrounding agricultural and milling industries. A bonus room at the lower level walkout allows easy access to the community center next door.

The memory care household offers an open and airy environment for 20 residents requiring cognitive assistance. Open and direct access to a porch and backyard provide the opportunity to experience the natural environment.

1

2

Site location	Small town
Site area	3.04 acres/132,200 square feet
Capacity	42 assisted living units;
	20 special care for persons
	with dementia
Total project cost	$6.4 M

Major design objectives and responses

Serve the increasing need for senior housing and services within a small rural community
Develop an affordable assisted living model that provides housing and services for both frail seniors and those needing specialized dementia care.

Create a facility that will be attractive to small town residents and blend into the existing community
Utilize understated, yet familiar residential building forms and materials that present an image of value without being overly expensive. Integrate products and imagery from local farming and milling industries.

Maintain a sense of belonging and connection to the greater community
Locate common areas and a trellised patio overlooking the main road into town. Provide easy walking access to the adjacent community center.

Create an active and comfortable environment for residents
Provide a flow and openness among common areas that create a critical mass of activities, within an appropriate hierarchy of spaces.

3

4

5

1   *Entrance*
2   *Memory care backyard*
3   *Trellis patio*
4   *Entry court*
5   *View from main road*

6

7

8

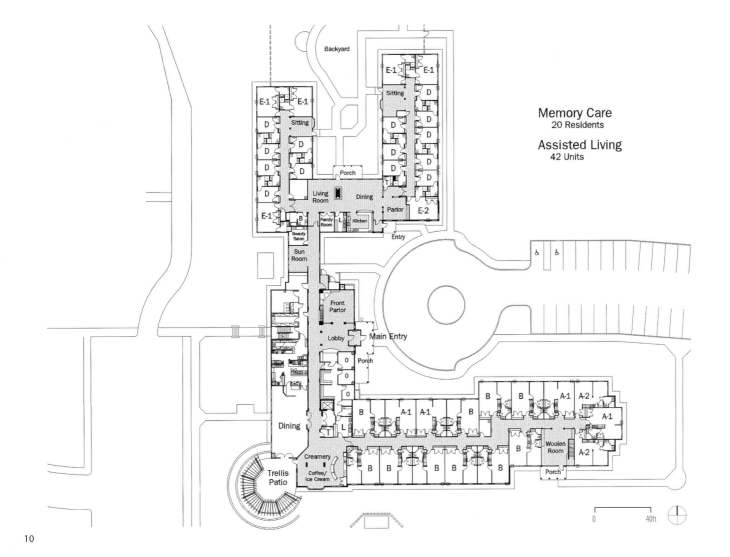

6 Memory care dining area
  with living area beyond
7 Creamery
8 Game room
9 Second floor plan
10 First floor plan

9

Memory Care
20 Residents

Assisted Living
42 Units

10

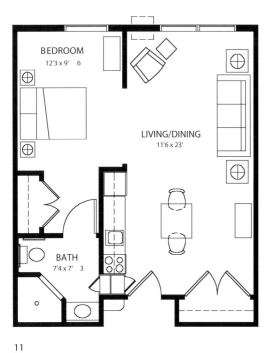

BEDROOM
12'3 x 9' 6

LIVING/DINING
11'6 x 23'

BATH
7'4 x 7' 3

11

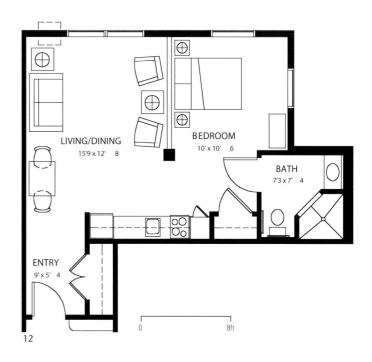

LIVING/DINING
15'9 x 12' 8

BEDROOM
10' x 10' 6

BATH
7'3 x 7' 4

ENTRY
9' x 5' 4

0   8ft

12

13

14

11,12,15,16 *Typical unit floor plans*

13 *Front parlor*

14 *Lobby*

17 *Woolen Room*

Photography: *Dave Olsen Photography*

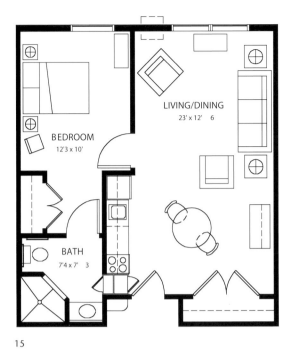

BEDROOM
12'3 x 10'

LIVING/DINING
23' x 12'   6

BATH
7'4 x 7'   3

15

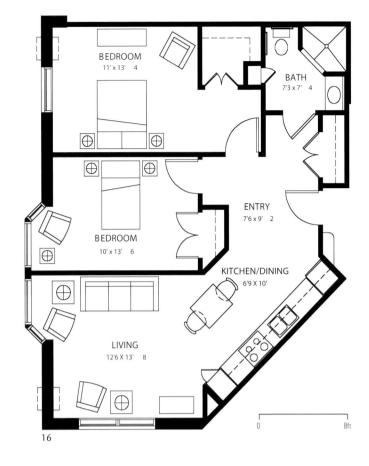

BEDROOM
11' x 13'   4

BATH
7'3 x 7'   4

ENTRY
7'6 x 9'   2

BEDROOM
10' x 13'   6

KITCHEN/DINING
6'9 X 10'

LIVING
12'6 X 13'   8

0   8ft

16

17

MIRAMONT POINTE

CLACKAMAS, OREGON

LRS Architects, Inc. / Associate architect: John B. Goodman Partnership

Architect's statement

This is a closed-in suburban care facility adjacent to three major population areas. The original concept was intended to be a two- to three-story facility that provided a continuum of care. Site complexities, slope, and significant wetlands created a design that was considerably more compact and vertical than was originally anticipated. The 154-unit facility is on eight levels that are diminished in scale due to a site that slopes away from the main roadway and entry. The facility is entered on the third level, which contains most of the major common areas, including the main kitchen, dining room, and some assisted/independent residences. Level one is devoted to memory care and features a memory/wandering garden. Level two houses assisted living residents while levels four to six house assisted/independent residents. The assisted/independent suite residents occupy levels seven and eight and are provided with upgraded interiors, finishes, and concierge service.

Site location	Suburban
Site area	5.6 acres/244,267 square feet
Capacity	140 assisted living units;
	14 special care for persons
	with dementia
Total project cost	Owner withheld

2

Major design objectives

Create an active facility that would attract educated and sophisticated upper-income senior residents.

Create a variety of living units with a diversity of care from which residents or their families can choose.

Create a community that provides educational opportunities for ongoing resident learning.

Upscale sizing and detailing of units.

Maximize views for all residents.

Create a local traditional resort atmosphere.

Create a long-term care facility that reflects the local vernacular and endures the test of time.

Integrate the outdoor spaces with a safe trail system that works in harmony and connects with the trailhead that leads to the natural environment.

3

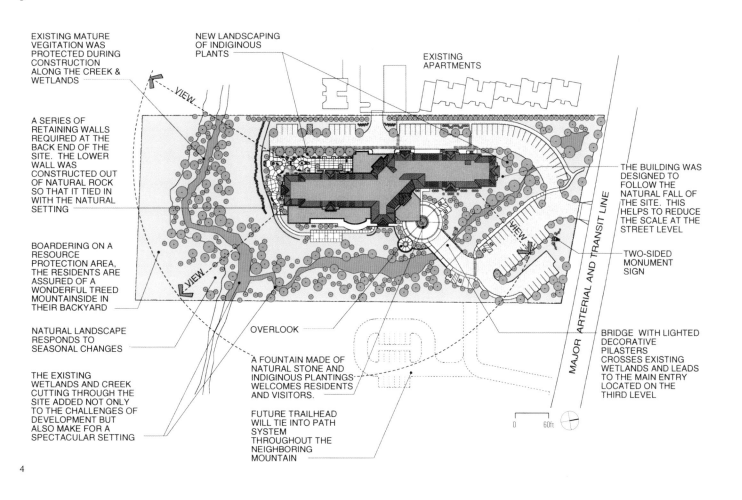

4

EXISTING MATURE VEGITATION WAS PROTECTED DURING CONSTRUCTION ALONG THE CREEK & WETLANDS

NEW LANDSCAPING OF INDIGINOUS PLANTS

EXISTING APARTMENTS

A SERIES OF RETAINING WALLS REQUIRED AT THE BACK END OF THE SITE. THE LOWER WALL WAS CONSTRUCTED OUT OF NATURAL ROCK SO THAT IT TIED IN WITH THE NATURAL SETTING

BOARDERING ON A RESOURCE PROTECTION AREA, THE RESIDENTS ARE ASSURED OF A WONDERFUL TREED MOUNTAINSIDE IN THEIR BACKYARD

NATURAL LANDSCAPE RESPONDS TO SEASONAL CHANGES

THE EXISTING WETLANDS AND CREEK CUTTING THROUGH THE SITE ADDED NOT ONLY TO THE CHALLENGES OF DEVELOPMENT BUT ALSO MAKE FOR A SPECTACULAR SETTING

OVERLOOK

A FOUNTAIN MADE OF NATURAL STONE AND INDIGINOUS PLANTINGS WELCOMES RESIDENTS AND VISITORS.

FUTURE TRAILHEAD WILL TIE INTO PATH SYSTEM THROUGHOUT THE NEIGHBORING MOUNTAIN

THE BUILDING WAS DESIGNED TO FOLLOW THE NATURAL FALL OF THE SITE. THIS HELPS TO REDUCE THE SCALE AT THE STREET LEVEL

TWO-SIDED MONUMENT SIGN

MAJOR ARTERIAL AND TRANSIT LINE

BRIDGE WITH LIGHTED DECORATIVE PILASTERS CROSSES EXISTING WETLANDS AND LEADS TO THE MAIN ENTRY LOCATED ON THE THIRD LEVEL

VIEW

0   60ft

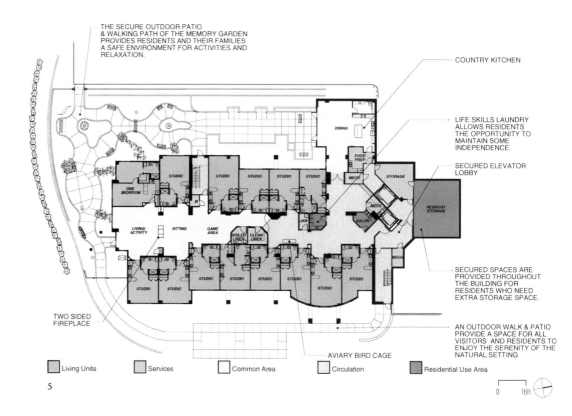

THE SECURE OUTDOOR PATIO & WALKING PATH OF THE MEMORY GARDEN PROVIDES RESIDENTS AND THEIR FAMILIES A SAFE ENVIRONMENT FOR ACTIVITIES AND RELAXATION.

COUNTRY KITCHEN

LIFE SKILLS LAUNDRY ALLOWS RESIDENTS THE OPPORTUNITY TO MAINTAIN SOME INDEPENDENCE.

SECURED ELEVATOR LOBBY

SECURED SPACES ARE PROVIDED THROUGHOUT THE BUILDING FOR RESIDENTS WHO NEED EXTRA STORAGE SPACE.

TWO SIDED FIREPLACE

AN OUTDOOR WALK & PATIO PROVIDE A SPACE FOR ALL VISITORS AND RESIDENTS TO ENJOY THE SERENITY OF THE NATURAL SETTING

AVIARY BIRD CAGE

Living Units   Services   Common Area   Circulation   Residential Use Area

0   16ft

5

6

7

8

9

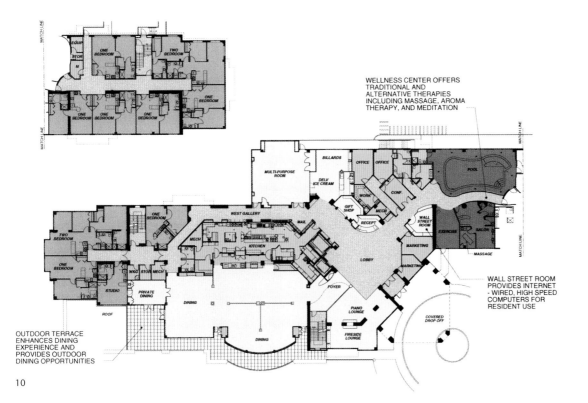

WELLNESS CENTER OFFERS
TRADITIONAL AND
ALTERNATIVE THERAPIES
INCLUDING MASSAGE, AROMA
THERAPY, AND MEDITATION

WALL STREET ROOM
PROVIDES INTERNET
- WIRED, HIGH SPEED
COMPUTERS FOR
RESIDENT USE

OUTDOOR TERRACE
ENHANCES DINING
EXPERIENCE AND
PROVIDES OUTDOOR
DINING OPPORTUNITIES

10

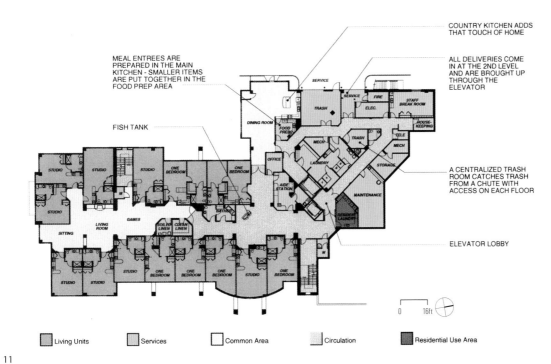

COUNTRY KITCHEN ADDS
THAT TOUCH OF HOME

MEAL ENTREES ARE
PREPARED IN THE MAIN
KITCHEN - SMALLER ITEMS
ARE PUT TOGETHER IN THE
FOOD PREP AREA

ALL DELIVERIES COME
IN AT THE 2ND LEVEL
AND ARE BROUGHT UP
THROUGH THE
ELEVATOR

FISH TANK

A CENTRALIZED TRASH
ROOM CATCHES TRASH
FROM A CHUTE WITH
ACCESS ON EACH FLOOR

ELEVATOR LOBBY

0   16ft

■ Living Units   ■ Services   □ Common Area   ▨ Circulation   ■ Residential Use Area

11

5   First floor plan

6   Entry level, main lobby

7   Entry level, gallery

8   Entry level, fireside lounge and lobby

9   Memory care level, country kitchen

10   Third floor plan

11   Second floor plan

12

13

14

12 Entry level, main dining room
13 Assisted living/independent suites level,
    concierge, and entertainment room area
14 Fireside lounge and library
15 Entry level, wheelchair-accessible pool at
    wellness center
16 Assisted living/independent one bedroom unit,
    living room, and kitchen

Photography: SkyShots (3); Randy Shelton (1,2);
Holly Stickley (6–9,12–14,16); LRS Architects, Inc. (15)

15

16

SUNRISE OF LA JOLLA

La Jolla, California
Mithun

Architect's statement

The architects were challenged with the task of designing a unique 50-unit assisted living community that enhances the quality of lifestyle available for seniors on the former site of a one-story branch bank.

The goal was accomplished by creating an urban building solution, one where residents feel comfortable in close proximity to busy shops and restaurants, and abundant pedestrian and automobile traffic. From the upper floors, residents in west and north-facing rooms enjoy views of the Pacific Ocean.

The aesthetic of the building embraces the California mission-style with deep-set wood windows in thick stucco walls. The compact three-story building with underground garage expresses a clear sense of arrival and an appropriate fit into the neighborhood.

2

1

Site location	Urban
Site area	0.46 acres/20,228 square feet
Capacity	31 assisted living units;
	19 special care for persons
	with dementia
Total project cost	Not known

3

4

Major design objectives and responses

Create a high-quality residential environment in an urban mixed-use oceanfront neighborhood

From the upper floors, there are views to the Pacific Ocean from every room facing west and north. Quality materials used include clad wood windows and doors, integral colored stucco exterior, detailed roof eaves, and a barrel tile roof in the spirit of traditional building materials in the regional mission-style. Ample glazing and porches encourage outdoor excursions by emphasizing the relationship between the indoor rooms and outdoor gardens.

Maintain exterior and interior relationship

To create a familiar residential atmosphere and carry through the consideration to detail, special attention was paid to the interior detailing such as a wood staircase, crown moldings, base and chair rail trim, mission-style furnishings, and a selection of warm colors.

Transition from a commercial to a residential neighborhood

During the planning stages, an assisted living project was considered appropriate by city planners for this commercial zoned site. It would front the commercial context of the street, being comfortably close to the sidewalk, with common areas at the first floor that exhibit larger windows, furnishings, and lighting, indicative of a small carriage hotel. Directly uphill from the site are several multifamily and single family structures.

5

6

1   Upper floor living room with ocean view
2   Overview of project at intersection
3   Grand foyer with dining room beyond
4   Sunroom
5   Alzheimer's dining room and kitchen
6   Two-room studio unit

Common Areas
Office/Staff Circulation
Service
Residential Support
Assisted Living Units

SERVICE RAMP
DN

RAMP TO PARKING
DN

STUDIO
PATIO

MAINT. OFFICE
TRASH/ RECYCLE
DELIVERIES
STAFF LOUNGE
ELEC.

STAIR "B"
UP DN

STUDIO

PRIVATE DINING
TOILET

DINING ROOM

VEST.
TOILET
KITCHEN

STUDIO

STUDIO

CORRIDOR

PATIO

ELEV. A
ELEV. B

UP

HALLWAY

GRAND FOYER

ELEV. LOBBY

STUDIO

VEST.

ENTRANCE

CONCIERGE

EXEC. DIRECTOR

DRY STORAGE

STUDIO

BISTRO

SERVERY

FOYER

PATIO

WORK ROOM

HSKPG.

TOILET

STAIR "A"

PARLOR

MARKETING

3 SEASON PORCH

SMOKING PORCH

ONE BEDROOM

ACCESS. STUDIO

STUDIO

TWO BDRM.

PATIO

0   32ft

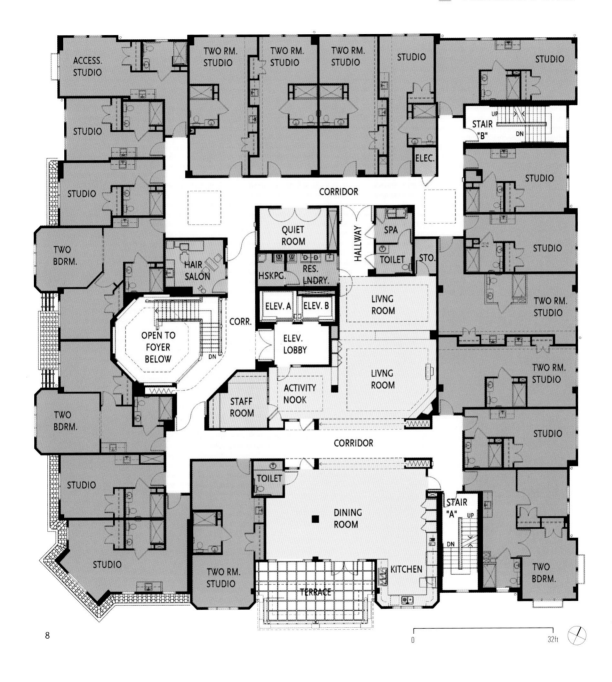

Common Areas

Office/Staff Circulation

Service

Residential Support

Alzheimer's Units

ACCESS. STUDIO

TWO RM. STUDIO

TWO RM. STUDIO

TWO RM. STUDIO

STUDIO

STUDIO

STUDIO

STAIR "B"
UP
DN

ELEC.

STUDIO

CORRIDOR

QUIET ROOM

HALLWAY

SPA

TWO BDRM.

HAIR SALON

HSKPG.

RES. LNDRY.

TOILET

STO.

STUDIO

STUDIO

LIVNG ROOM

TWO RM. STUDIO

OPEN TO FOYER BELOW
DN

CORR.

ELEV. A

ELEV. B

ELEV. LOBBY

LIVNG ROOM

TWO RM. STUDIO

TWO BDRM.

STAFF ROOM

ACTIVITY NOOK

CORRIDOR

STUDIO

STUDIO

TOILET

DINING ROOM

STAIR "A"
UP
DN

STUDIO

TWO RM. STUDIO

TERRACE

KITCHEN

TWO BDRM.

8

0   32ft

7   First floor plan

8   Second floor plan

Photography: Architectural Photography, Inc.

THE SYLVESTERY AT VINSON HALL

McLEAN, VIRGINIA

Reese, Lower, Patrick & Scott, Ltd.

Architect's statement

The Sylvestery was designed to support its 'Free to Be' program. This encourages resident freedom and choice in a safe, residential scaled environment. The design specifically addresses environmental therapy and the positive impact of strong connections to nature and daylight.

The project's most unique feature is four internal gardens, each with a distinct appearance and function. Single-loaded corridors allow continuous viewing into the gardens, providing a bright, naturally lit community that visually and physically dissolves barriers to the outside. Residents are free to walk in and out of the secured garden areas. Exterior building materials such as brick and trellises are used inside the building to further emphasize the outdoor connections.

Resident rooms are private and each bathroom includes a European-style shower for a more dignified approach to bathing. A beauty shop, boutique, craft room, solarium and remote café are scattered throughout the facility to promote resident movement and exploration.

1

2

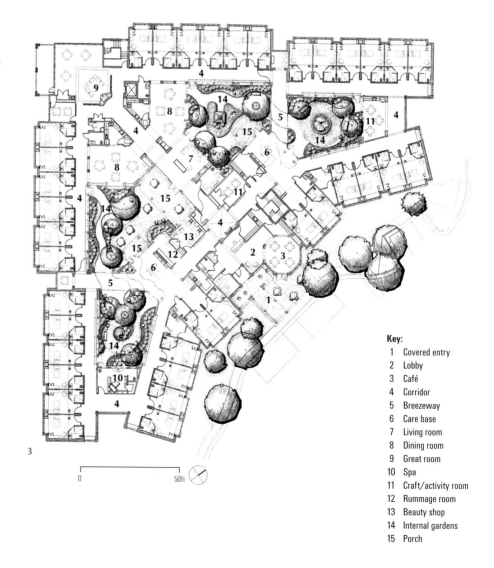

3

1&2   *Exterior view*

3   *Overall floor plan*

4&5   *'Free to be' statue in courtyard*

6   *Dementia courtyard*

Site location	Suburban
Site area	2.5 acres/109,147 square feet
Capacity	36 special care for persons with dementia
Total project cost	$9.3 M

Key:
1   Covered entry
2   Lobby
3   Café
4   Corridor
5   Breezeway
6   Care base
7   Living room
8   Dining room
9   Great room
10   Spa
11   Craft/activity room
12   Rummage room
13   Beauty shop
14   Internal gardens
15   Porch

0   50ft

4

5

6

Major design objectives and responses

Provide a safe environment that allows residents with memory loss to wander freely and safely

Strategically placed care bases allow staff to discreetly monitor gardens and social spaces. Glass walled corridors provide a seamless view into the four gardens and encourage residents to independently venture outdoors. The floor plan provides a natural looping circulation pattern with strategically placed destination points of various program spaces.

Deinstitutionalize the floor plan and create a residential, homelike environment

Long, double-loaded corridors are avoided throughout the plan. Living rooms, dining rooms, great rooms, and libraries are open to the halls, further diminishing the sense of corridors. Porches, fireplaces, window seats, interior windows, and country kitchens all reinforce the homelike setting.

Provide a building that does not feel institutional from the exterior

The 36-bed facility was broken down into a series of smaller connected houses. Each cluster of six private rooms creates a house-scaled element defined by its own roof and brick gabled ends with chimneys.

Maximize the connection to the outdoors to improve resident wellbeing

The layout of six houses creates the four gardens and provides an overall floor plan where residents are always connected to nature and the outdoors. The four gardens become the ever-changing interior design or wallpaper of the corridors.

Provide rooms that address privacy, minimize incontinence, and allow easy staff monitoring

The design strategically places the bed where the resident has a direct view out of a large window, as well as a view directly to the toilet in the bathroom, serving as a cueing device to lessen incontinence. The headboard of the bed is placed on the wall directly in front of the entry door, which allows staff members to easily monitor residents in their rooms. For additional privacy, a low cabinet with a decorative column is placed between the bed and the door.

8

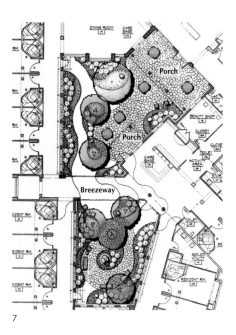

7   9

7   Courtyard concepts
8   Beauty shop
9   Corridor with connection to outdoors
10   Floor plan showing care base/visual control
11   Living room

0   50ft

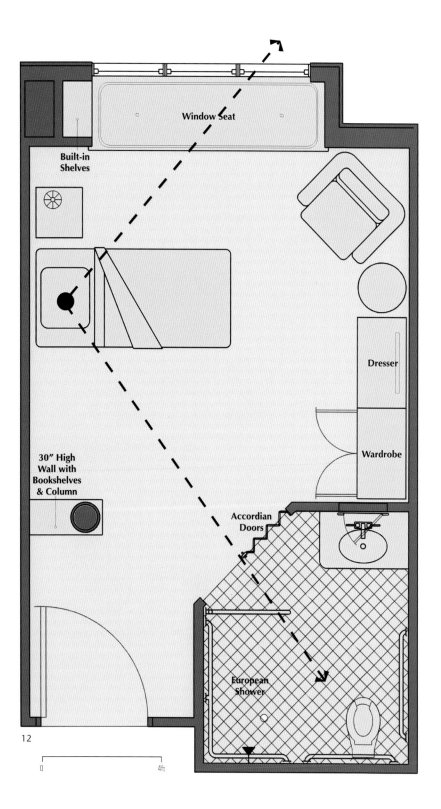

Window Seat

Built-in
Shelves

30" High
Wall with
Bookshelves
& Column

Accordian
Doors

Dresser

Wardrobe

European
Shower

12

0   4ft

13

12 *Typical private room floor plan*

13 *Resident room*

14 *Spa*

Photography: *Larry Lefever Photography*

14

DESIGN FOR

NURSING FACILITY

GING REVIEW

Citation

Using a household concept, this nursing residence explores intimate care provisions and what may be a new model for the nursing environment. Economies in building construction may offset this costlier but more personal staffing approach. The simplicity and straightforwardness of the facility design are a credit to the foresight shown in the collaboration between client, staff, and designer.

THE GREEN HOUSES AT TRACEWAY™ TUPELO, MISSISSIPPI

The McCarty Company–Design Group, P.A.

Architect's statement

The project mission was to replace an aging skilled nursing facility and begin a global change in the way that skilled care is delivered to elders. Rooted in the Eden Alternative™ principles, the new concept demanded smaller buildings with the warmth of home, the creative use of technology and the opportunity for regular contact with living things. Phase 1 consists of four 6,000-square-foot homes for ten elders each. Uniquely trained staff manage the household and meet the care needs of each elder. Treatment needs are met by a clinical support team, visiting each home, making house calls as needed. The result is a home environment where frail elders receive highly skilled care and experience variety and spontaneity as they are intimately touched by the rich sights, sounds, and smells of everyday life 'at home.'

1&2 *Exterior view featuring residential style, patio, and porch area*
3 *Site plan*

1

2

Site location	Small town
Site area	13.9 acres/608,563 square feet
Capacity	56 cottages/villas; 40 skilled nursing care beds
Total project cost	$3.2 M

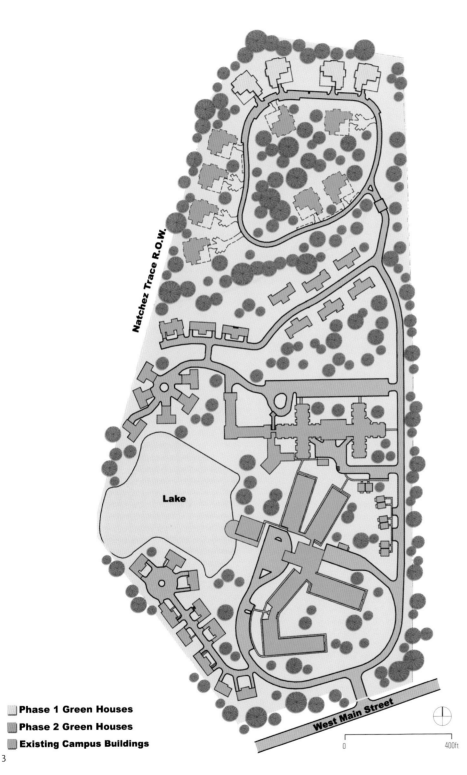

Phase 1 Green Houses
Phase 2 Green Houses
Existing Campus Buildings

Natchez Trace R.O.W.

Lake

West Main Street

0   400ft

Major design objectives and responses

Create a small home environment where frail elders can live and grow while receiving skilled care

Each building is a warm and friendly home with an open-plan living space called 'the hearth.' It includes a full-functioning kitchen, where all meals are prepared, and a long family-style dining table for 12. There is an abundance of natural light with views of the wooded surroundings across the accessible patio/garden. Beyond the (electric) fireplace, wood trim and comfortable furnishings, lies the technical and clinical functionality of a licensed skilled nursing environment, all cleverly concealed from view.

Provide each elder with a private room and bath

Opening directly onto 'the hearth' are ten private rooms, with private bathrooms that include showers.

Protect the natural habitat of the site

Smaller buildings and limited parking helped to retain this naturally wooded site. All buildings, drives, and underground utilities were strategically placed to protect trees and the natural landscape.

Meet all state regulatory requirements

With the concept being somewhat unusual by nursing home standards, strict compliance with all licensure requirements was a clear objective, even in this home environment. The project team explored creative ways to meet the intent of each requirement, and with much support and cooperation from the State Department of Licensure, no variances were requested or required.

4

5

6

4 Hearth with elder rooms in background
5 Hearth and kitchen dining area
6 Elder room featuring private room,
   private bath, and lift system
7 Floor plan
Photography: *Jeffrey Jacobs/Architectural
Photo, Inc.*
Floor plan: *The McCarty Company-Design
Group, P.A.*

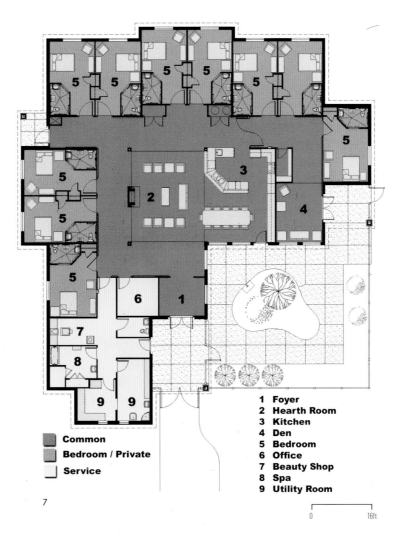

Common
Bedroom / Private
Service

1 **Foyer**
2 **Hearth Room**
3 **Kitchen**
4 **Den**
5 **Bedroom**
6 **Office**
7 **Beauty Shop**
8 **Spa**
9 **Utility Room**

7

0   16ft

The designer was guided by the client mission of addressing staffing issues (notably the use of space by different shifts) and thinking outside the box to stay within the budget. The design team paid particular attention to how the built environment and the care provision program interact, resulting in the understated vernacular dignity of the facility being achieved without loss of residential scale.

The State Veterans Home at Fitzsimons Aurora, Colorado

Boulder Associates, Inc. / Associate architect: Luis O. Acosta Architects

Architect's statement

The client's program called for a state-of-the-art 180-bed skilled nursing facility that provided maximum independence for the veterans living there, while optimizing staffing and other operational aspects to minimize expenses. Two 42-bed and two 48-bed nursing units were developed in a crenellated cluster design that features decentralized nurse-aide alcoves. Using a flexible, pager-enabled call system, cluster sizes are adjusted to fit staffing needs at each shift.

Only 20 of 180 beds were allowed to be private, so bi-axial and L-shaped double rooms with dividing walls were developed. Each resident has equal access to the corridor, toilet room, and windows. Bay windows with window seats increase usable space without exceeding maximum allowable room sizes. Resident toilet rooms feature oversized accordion doors, extra maneuvering space, and folding grab bars flanking the water closet for functional accessibility, exceeding ADA requirements.

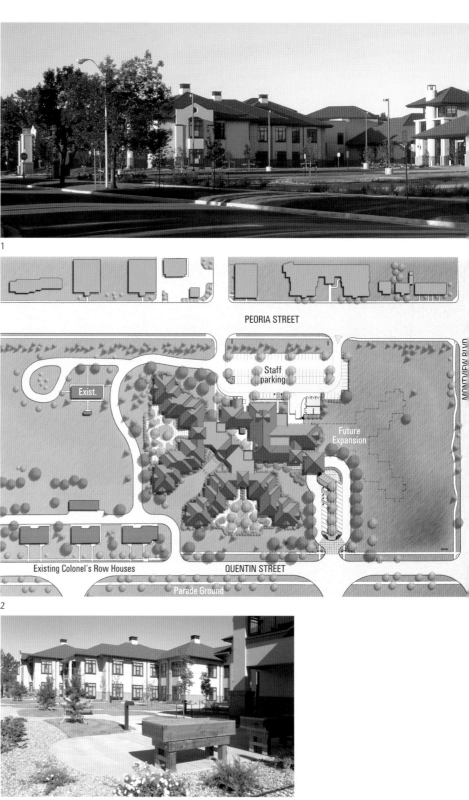

1

2

3

Site location	Urban
Site area	15 acres/653,400 square feet
Capacity	180 skilled nursing care beds
Total project cost	$24.84 M

Major design objectives and responses

Design for staffing efficiency

Considering that 80 percent of life cycle operating costs for the facility are for staff costs, the required 180 beds are divided into two 42-bed and two 48-bed units. Each unit is divided into six equal clusters with a CNA work area to allow one CNA per seven or eight residents during the day. Support and social areas are decentralized to reduce travel time for staff and time spent transporting residents. Dining rooms are paired so that a single serving pantry supplies food to two dining rooms.

Empower and enable residents to be as independent as possible

Decentralized family rooms and dining rooms reduce travel distances. Rooms are designed for flexibility in bed and furniture placement, allowing residents to customize their rooms. The toilet room design is another example that enables independence in residents.

Maximize privacy for residents

Individual bay windows and thermostats eliminate the need for residents to intrude into their roommate's space. The toilet rooms have oversized accordion-type doors, with two extra accordion panels, so that the door need not be pulled taut. Bathing suites are located near the midpoint of each leg of a unit, minimizing travel distances and avoiding the need for residents to pass by major public areas such as dining rooms or activity rooms, while the shower area has a separate drying area.

Design universal resident units for future flexibility

All four nursing units are designed to allow special populations, such as short-term rehabilitation or dementia care to be housed together, if desired. Each unit can be divided into as many as four sections, utilizing smoke barrier and area separation doors, allowing sub-units as small as 10 or 11 beds.

1   Overall view
2   Site plan
3   Outdoor garden
4   Exterior of main lobby
5   Courtyard

6

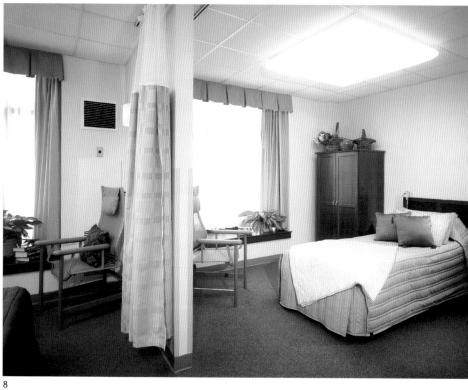

7

8

6   *CNA desk*

7   *Family room and hallway*

8   *Shared room*

9   *Shared room floor plan*

10 *Family room*

11 *Private dining room*

12 *Private resident room*

Photography: *Ed LaCasse*

10

9

11

12

CARROLL CAMPBELL PLACE
ALZHEIMER'S UNIT LEXINGTON, SOUTH CAROLINA

Perkins & Will

Architect's statement

Carroll Campbell Place is a 24,500-square-foot Alzheimer's skilled nursing facility located on a primary approach road into its small town in South Carolina. Its site offers a unique opportunity to reinforce the image of coming home, both for local citizens driving past the building on their way into town, and for families and residents of CCP who understand it as an extension of their own homes. The over-arching goal of the design team is to convey the welcoming, personalized quality of its healthcare through residential massing, materials, and vernacular detailing.

Two 18-bed units of private rooms are arranged into T-shaped plans, each with common sitting room, living room, kitchen, dining area, craft area, and covered porches, easily overseen by central staff. Extensive gardens are accessible to residents 24 hours a day, extending continuous wandering paths in and out of the building. Alzheimer-specific details encourage resident independence and family interaction.

1

Site location	Small town
Site area	18.65 acres/812,394 square feet
Capacity	36 skilled nursing care beds
Total project cost	$6 M

2

1 *Porch, wandering garden, and water feature*
2 *Front entrance*
3 *Site plan*
4 *Porch outside resident sitting room*

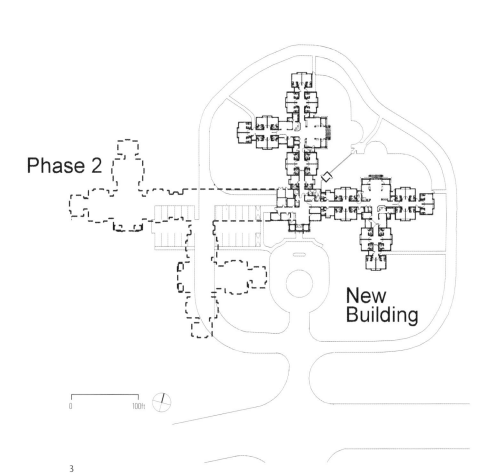

Phase 2

New
Building

0   100ft

3

Major design objectives and responses

Convey the unique philosophy of care through the exterior imagery

Traditional gabled roofs, bay windows, and trellised canopy effectively de-institutionalize the building.

Emphasize resident individuality and dignity

Reminiscence boxes, plate rails, deep window sills, window seat cupboards, custom wardrobes, and lockable closets provide space for personal belongings. Valuable items can be displayed out-of-reach or in locked glass cabinets.

Encourage independence

Rooms are laid out with clear sightlines between the bed and the water-closet to encourage independent toileting.

Bathrooms feature lights on motion sensors and automatic faucets and flushers.

Custom wardrobe cabinets in resident rooms include a cupboard in which each day's outfit is laid out the night before by staff; in the morning, the resident can dress independently.

Each wing is distinguished by its own color scheme. Non-resident rooms have doors and doorframes painted to blend in with the general corridor. Public areas have wooden handrails on carved brackets.

Encourage resident activity

Secure outdoor gardens are accessible to residents 24 hours a day. Potting sheds, porches, trellised benches, and moveable picnic tables provide a variety of activity areas.

Common spaces at the center of each unit include a kitchen, craft area with washer and dryer, dining room, sitting area, and living room, all supervisable from the staff area.

Aviaries and aquariums provide focal points for conversation.

Ensure resident safety and security

Entry from the building lobby into each unit is possible only through a set of doors controlled by keypad locks. Doors leading into gardens are equipped with gentle chimes. Support room doors and cabinetry inappropriate for residents are locked.

4

6

Opposite   *Shared sitting room*

6   *Wandering garden*
     with moveable seating

7   *Building plan*

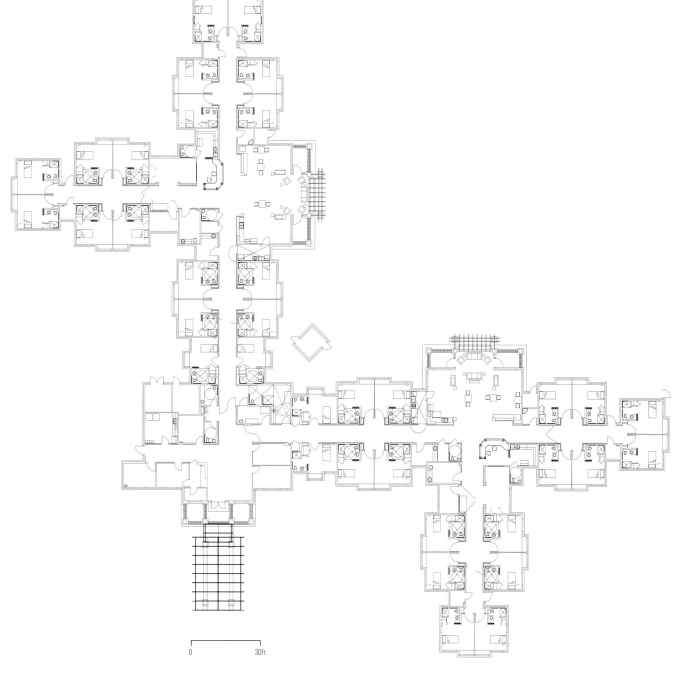

7

0   30ft

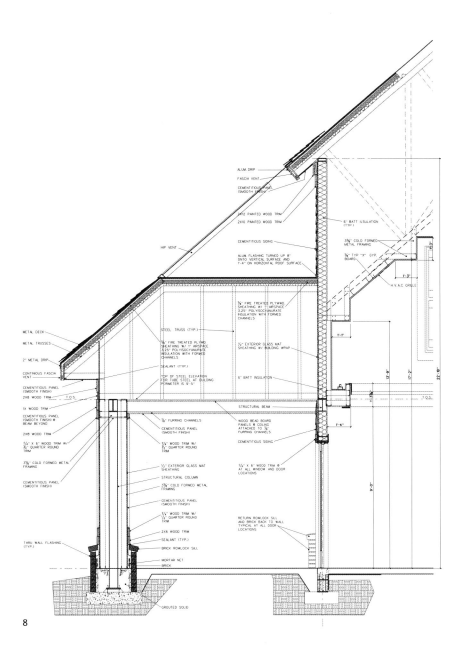

ALUM. DRIP

FASCIA VENT

CEMENTITIOUS PANEL (SMOOTH FINISH)

2X12 PAINTED WOOD TRIM

2X10 PAINTED WOOD TRIM

6" BATT INSULATION (TYP.)

HIP VENT

CEMENTITIOUS SIDING

3⅝" COLD FORMED METAL FRAMING

ALUM. FLASHING TURNED UP 8" ONTO VERTICAL SURFACE AND 1'-4" ON HORIZONTAL ROOF SURFACE

⅝" TYP "X" GYP. BOARD

H.V.A.C. GRILLE

METAL DECK

STEEL TRUSS (TYP.)

⅝" FIRE TREATED PLYWD. SHEATHING W/ 1" AIRSPACE 3.25" POLYISOCYANURATE INSULATION WITH FORMED CHANNELS

METAL TRUSSES

2" METAL DRIP

⅝" FIRE TREATED PLYWD. SHEATHING W/ 1" AIRSPACE 3.25" POLYISOCYANURATE INSULATION WITH FORMED CHANNELS

CONTINUOUS FASCIA VENT

½" EXTERIOR GLASS MAT SHEATHING W/ BUILDING WRAP

CEMENTITIOUS PANEL (SMOOTH FINISH)

TOP OF STEEL ELEVATION FOR TUBE STEEL AT BUILDING PERIMETER IS 9'-5"

6" BATT INSULATION

2X8 WOOD TRIM

T.O.S.

1X WOOD TRIM

CEMENTITIOUS PANEL (SMOOTH FINISH) @ BEAM BEYOND

⅞" FURRING CHANNELS

STRUCTURAL BEAM

2X8 WOOD TRIM

CEMENTITIOUS PANEL (SMOOTH FINISH)

WOOD BEAD BOARD PANELS @ CEILING ATTACHED TO ⅞" FURRING CHANNELS

1½" X 6" WOOD TRIM W/ ¾" QUARTER ROUND TRIM

1¼" WOOD TRIM W/ ¾" QUARTER ROUND TRIM

CEMENTITIOUS SIDING

3⅝" COLD FORMED METAL FRAMING

½" EXTERIOR GLASS MAT SHEATHING

1¼" X 6" WOOD TRIM @ AT ALL WINDOW AND DOOR LOCATIONS

CEMENTITIOUS PANEL (SMOOTH FINISH)

STRUCTURAL COLUMN

3⅝" COLD FORMED METAL FRAMING

CEMENTITIOUS PANEL (SMOOTH FINISH)

1¼" WOOD TRIM W/ ¾" QUARTER ROUND TRIM

2X6 WOOD TRIM

RETURN ROWLOCK SILL AND BRICK BACK TO WALL TYPICAL AT ALL DOOR LOCATIONS

SEALANT (TYP.)

THRU WALL FLASHING (TYP.)

BRICK ROWLOCK SILL

MORTAR NET

BRICK

GROUTED SOLID

8

9

10

11

12

8 *Building section through porch and sitting area*

9 *Shared sitting area*

10 *Resident room*

11 *Grouped resident room entries*

12 *Dining room*

13 *Detail of wooden handrail*

Photography: *Cameron Triggs (1,2,4,5,9,11–13);*

Larry Campbell (6,10)

13

ABRAMSON CENTER FOR JEWISH LIFE

HORSHAM, PENNSYLVANIA

EwingCole / Associate architect: Nelson-Tremain Partnership

Architect's statement

Using the family home as an inspiration for both architecture and organization, the facility features The Residence, The Inn and Town Square. Each area was designed to create a space unique to its occupants while generating an overall sense of community.

The Residence design is based on a 'household' module of 27 residents, grouped in three clusters that foster privacy and independence while enabling residents to enjoy common areas. Two households form a villa of 54 residents. Neighborhoods encompass the villas, which share common areas that incorporate displays of Jewish art.

The Inn houses older adults who require assistance with the demands of daily life. It includes private studios and one-bedroom suites, specially designed living and dining areas, and access to comprehensive geriatric care.

The Town Square is a striking interior community space with an exterior scale and ambiance that links The Residence and The Inn, and features a synagogue, beauty and barber shop, children's play alcove and technology center.

1

2

Site location	Suburban
Site area	41 acres/1,785,967 square feet
Capacity	48 assisted living units; 324 skilled nursing care beds
Total project cost	$70.7 M

1 Main entry approach view
2 Porte-cochere at entry
3 Town square garden adjacent to synagogue
4 Entry porches

3

4

Major design objectives and responses

Create a positive social life and milieu

The Residence and The Inn offer a variety of socialization and gathering spaces including:

- dining and larger living rooms serving 24–29 residents
- home-scaled, more private dens for groups of 9–12 residents
- lobby, clubroom, and private dining spaces in the more public main entry areas
- the Town Square atrium is activated by gift shop, technology center, art gallery, therapy areas, outpatient doctor's office, community meeting rooms and the synagogue

Blend nature and the outdoors into everyday living

- circulation in The Residence and The Inn leads to destination spaces with natural light
- the building plans and massing form four garden courtyards, each with a distinct design
- the skylight atrium of Town Square brings the outdoors indoors and provides an all-season, outdoor-scaled space, easily accessible to residents and families

Adapt to changing needs

- adjacent resident rooms in the nursing home will have provisions for adding an interconnecting door for couples' suites
- one-bedroom assisted living apartments can be easily converted to two-bedroom suites with shared bathroom and kitchenette
- the dens in each of the household clusters lend themselves to dining at a small scale
- the Residence and The Inn are anticipating aging-in-place, resulting in a high percentage of physically frail residents with some form of dementia
- the site has preserved 31 acres for future development

Promote health and wellbeing

- bathrooms, including fold-down grab bars, specifically designed for elderly use with varying levels of staff assistance
- corridor handrails designed for gripping/ mobility and leaning/resting
- frequently spaced furnished alcoves to encourage residents to walk and rest

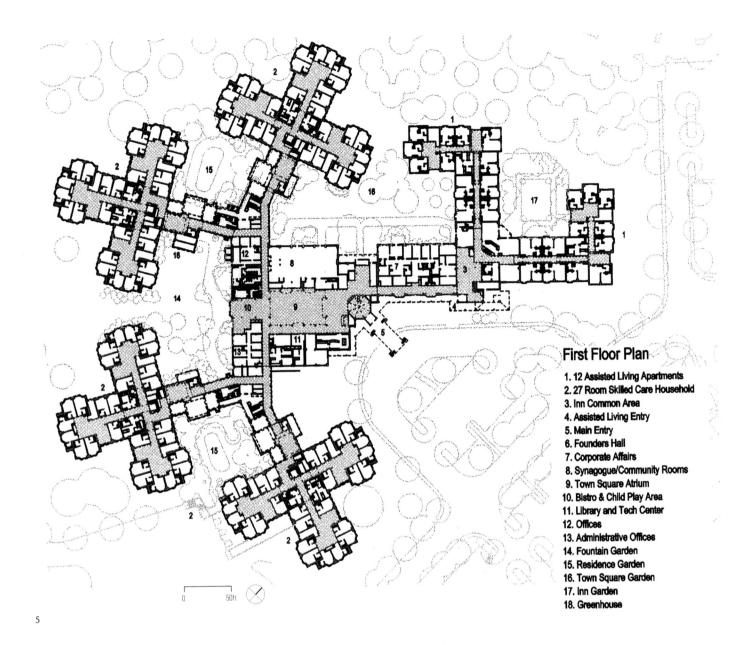

First Floor Plan

1. 12 Assisted Living Apartments
2. 27 Room Skilled Care Household
3. Inn Common Area
4. Assisted Living Entry
5. Main Entry
6. Founders Hall
7. Corporate Affairs
8. Synagogue/Community Rooms
9. Town Square Atrium
10. Bistro & Child Play Area
11. Library and Tech Center
12. Offices
13. Administrative Offices
14. Fountain Garden
15. Residence Garden
16. Town Square Garden
17. Inn Garden
18. Greenhouse

0   50ft

5

6

7

5 First floor plan
6 Typical villa
7 Residence garden at villas
8 Dining room
9 Town square, main central space with skylight
10 Mosaic artwork at synagogue entrance

8

9

10

11

12

13

14

11 *Resident living room*

12 *Bedroom*

13 *Porch*

14 *Resident bathroom*

15 *Staff areas at cluster dens*

Photography: *Jeffrey Totaro*

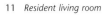

15

Brewster Village

APPLETON, WISCONSIN

Horty Elving

1

Architect's statement

Optimizing quality of life for residents and staff motivated the design response for this project. The population includes people with chronic mental illness, mental retardation, dementias, developmental disabilities, and the elderly with medical care needs. It is designed to easily adapt to future changes in resident demographics.

Physical, psychological, and emotional wellbeing for residents and staff is central—providing life experiences as similar as possible to life outside the Village. Each resident has a private room with a private toilet, which is part of a household where domestic activities including dining, bathing, and personal laundry occur. Households are grouped into five neighborhoods located around a town center community space, offering opportunities for shopping, working, learning, and worshipping. A sense of self, as well as a relationship with a greater community is fundamental to wellbeing.

2

Site location	Small town
Site area	Not known
Capacity	204 skilled nursing care beds
Total project cost	$24.1 M

3   4

Major design objectives and responses

Quality of life for residents and staff

Overall design promotes wellbeing of residents, and is carried through details (for example, the secure courtyards for each household allow fresh air and sunlight within a more intimate setting and easier access to residents).

Staffing efficiency

Decentralized functions ease staff workload.

Promoting a sense of home, within a greater sense of community

Offering residents a fuller spectrum of life experiences within the safety of the facility.

Safety of residents and staff

Decentralized domestic activities reduce institutional feel, and feels more homelike.

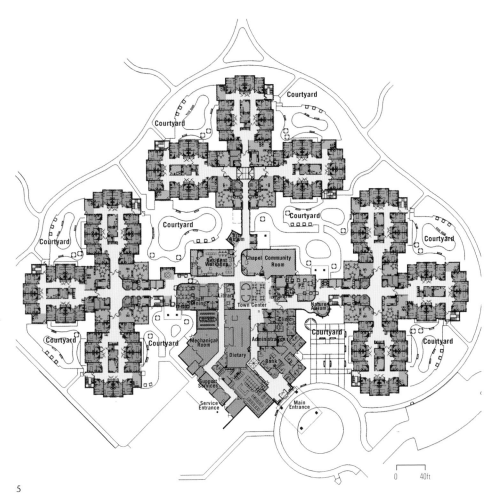

5

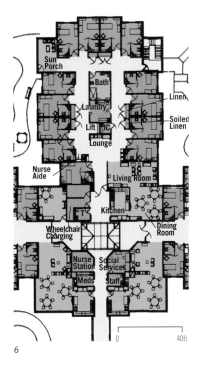

1   Overall facility exterior

2   Exterior from within courtyard

3   Family area/sitting room, with
    entrance to outdoor courtyard

4   Town center

5   First floor plan

6   Household floor plan

6

7

9

8

Photography: *Viken Djaferian, Fotografix*

10

11

12

Carleton–Willard Village Nursing & Retirement Center BEDFORD, MASSACHUSETTS

Tsomides Associates Architects Planners/TAAP

Architect's statement

The revitalization of the nursing center included a reduction of the existing 120-bed skilled nursing facility by 20 beds in order to accommodate new, vital program spaces. The first floor was transformed from a 40-bed SNF into a 30-bed special care Alzheimer's unit, with direct access to a large new sensory garden. Central nurse's stations and bathing rooms were relocated within each residential wing, as they were also on the second floor, providing a closer relationship between staff and residents. New resident lounges were created opposite each nurse's station, infusing the corridors with natural light. New activities rooms in a redesigned core area recapture the simple pleasures of the 1950s, and encourage and reassure residents. The second floor was transformed from two 40-bed units to 34 and 36-bed units, with new dining room and rehabilitation services created on the same level, eliminating the need to transport residents to programs previously located on the first floor.

1

2   3   4

Site location	Suburban
Site area	2.06 acres/89,600 square feet
Capacity	30 special care for persons with dementia; 70 skilled nursing care beds
Total project cost	$10.7 M

1   New second floor roof terrace
2   New sensory garden, view toward north wing
3   New exterior west elevation
4   Renovated private resident room
5   Existing first floor plan

6   Renovated first floor plan
7   1950's living room

Photography: Hutchins Photography, Inc. (1,3,4,7); Tsomides Associates Architects Planners/TAAP (2)

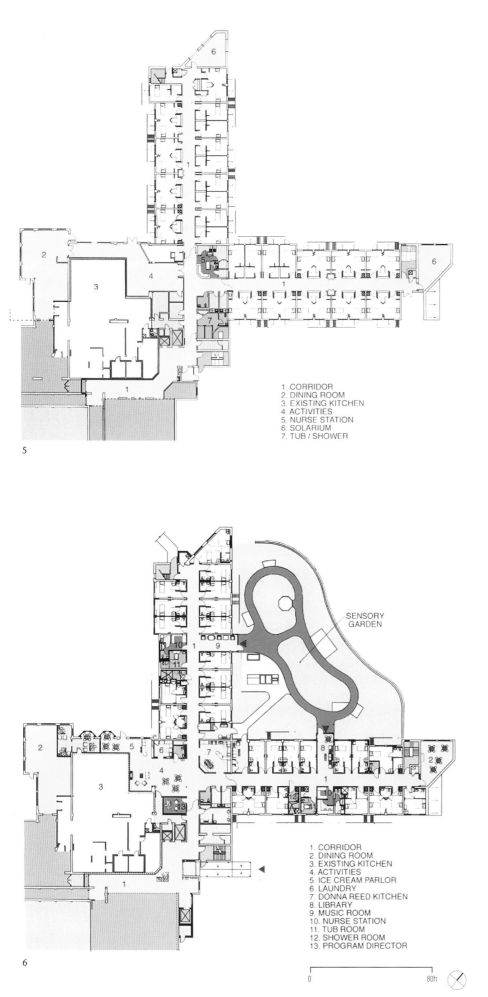

1. CORRIDOR
2. DINING ROOM
3. EXISTING KITCHEN
4. ACTIVITIES
5. NURSE STATION
6. SOLARIUM
7. TUB / SHOWER

5

SENSORY
GARDEN

1. CORRIDOR
2. DINING ROOM
3. EXISTING KITCHEN
4. ACTIVITIES
5. ICE CREAM PARLOR
6. LAUNDRY
7. DONNA REED KITCHEN
8. LIBRARY
9. MUSIC ROOM
10. NURSE STATION
11. TUB ROOM
12. SHOWER ROOM
13. PROGRAM DIRECTOR

6

0   80ft

Major design objectives and responses

Transform the institutional-type nursing unit into a homelike environment with improved operational efficiencies
Decentralized nurse's stations and bathing rooms are located within each bedroom wing, bringing staff, vital programs, and services closer to residents.

Recapture the 1950s to create a caring environment for Alzheimer's residents
The 1950's living room, ice cream parlor, Donna Reed kitchen and laundry provide a series of activities vital to the wellbeing of the residents.

Create a safe, secure, and stimulating outdoor environment
The new sensory garden with its serpentine cedar fence, wandering path loop, raised planters, and front porches provides these much-needed living experiences.

Reduce or eliminate the operational inefficiencies of transporting residents from one floor to another for dining and rehabilitation therapies
The second-floor nursing units have a new dining room, rehabilitation services, and an outdoor roof terrace located on the same level.

7

Hebrew Home of Greater Washington: Smith–Kogod Building Rockville, Maryland

Perkins Eastman

Architect's statement

The design reconfigured a fully-occupied 1970's style building with 282 skilled care residents, to create indoor and outdoor environments, address resident care and quality of life issues, provide non-institutional settings, and enhance the marketing of the facility. This project is part of a care continuum that includes 500 independent living units, 558 skilled care units, adult day care, a clinic, and a 60-unit assisted living residence which is under construction.

The design responds to the needs of residents, most of whom have some form of dementia. Outdated finishes, lighting, and floor plans characterized by long undifferentiated corridors contributed to an institutional character, as well as compromising staff efficiency, privacy and age-related sensory changes. The new layouts create resident and staff spaces that are varied in scale and character, allowing for flexibility in resident activities and staff efficiency, and provide a hierarchy of circulation to distinguish more public areas of the nursing unit. The reconfigured plan also distinguishes between public and private spaces for residents and staff, integrates the nurse station into surrounding common spaces, opens dining and activity rooms to natural light, and provides spaces for interaction between staff and residents.

The addition of a solarium room on all floors with a new elevator provides access to a large, secure garden that accommodates diverse experiences for residents and family members of all ages.

Resident rooms received improved lighting and finishes, as well as a new nurse call system with multiple locations in order to provide flexibility in bed and furniture placement, allowing residents freedom to utilize personal furnishings.

Site location	Suburban
Site area	6.2 acres/270,072 square feet
Capacity	282 skilled nursing care beds
Total project cost	$10.1 M

1

2

Major design objectives

Provide greater variety in resident common spaces, increase amount of daylight in dining and common spaces, and provide visibility through spaces to encourage socialization and allow for unobtrusive staff observation.

Provide stronger definition between public and private sectors by creating public corridor zones, with sitting areas and places for artwork display, to add interest and variety. Enhance resident privacy and dignity with upgrades to bathing areas; and new finishes, furnishings, and lighting in resident rooms.

Update lighting and finishes to create a more residential-like environment, with attention to enhanced illumination, reduction of glare, and attention to acoustics and furniture ergonomics appropriate to a frail population.

Support staff efficiency by providing a strong differentiation between work, meeting, and respite spaces.

In response to limited outdoor access, provide a garden and outdoor rooms that can accommodate a variety of activities, accessible to all four floors via an elevator and solarium addition.

3

4

1 *Resident common room with private dining and view to staff support area*
2 *Dining room with solarium addition*
3 *Social hall*
4 *Resident spa/bathing room*

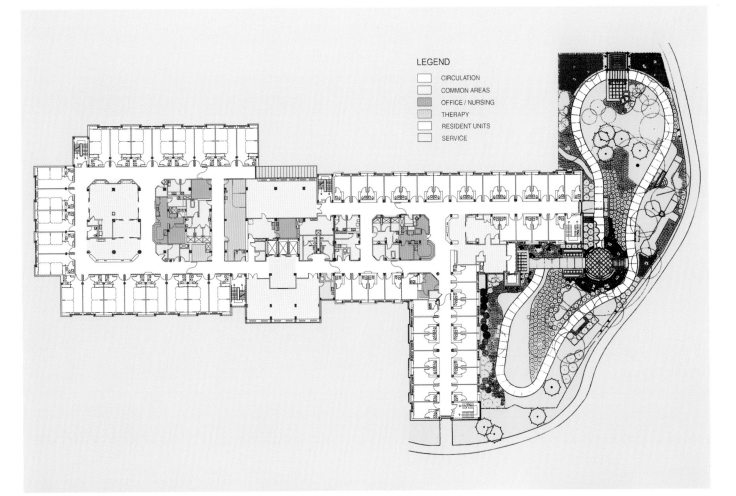

LEGEND

- CIRCULATION
- COMMON AREAS
- OFFICE / NURSING
- THERAPY
- RESIDENT UNITS
- SERVICE

6

7

8

5,7,8 *Garden*
6 *New floor plan*
Photography: *Edward Massery*

SUMMIT NURSING HOME

LYNCHBURG, VIRGINIA
Hughes Associates Architects

Architect's statement

The Summit Nursing Home provides four residential communities under one roof, while retaining a sense of shared township. Based on a similar facility that this team had pioneered, the architects found that investing in a sense of place paid off untold dividends. Residents can rest in their rooms or commit the day to capitalizing on the many features that the town has to offer. Residents can walk in and around the landscaped court and develop their own gardens in individual plots of ground. The Summit provides social spaces, activity pods, eating environments, and hair salons, leaving the resident with a sense of pride, dignity, and most importantly, a feeling of home.

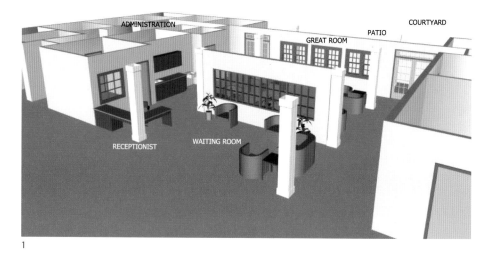

1

2

3

Site location	Suburban
Site area	9.9 acres
Capacity	120 skilled nursing care beds
Total project cost	$6 M

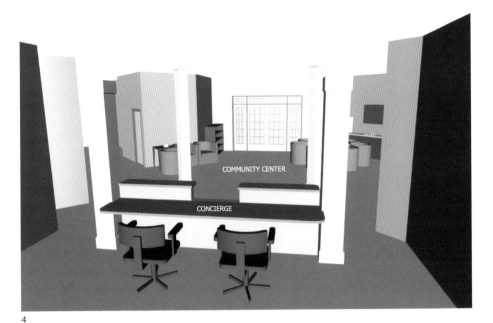

Major design objectives

- Create a sense of place (interior and exterior) that feels like a home, not just a house
- Create a facility that respects the resident
- Create a world of dignity celebrating the final chapter of one's life
- Create environments reflecting a sense of pride and ownership for resident, family, and staff
- Ask of oneself: what would I want if this were my home? In other words, treat the codes and guidelines as minimum, not maximum, standards

4

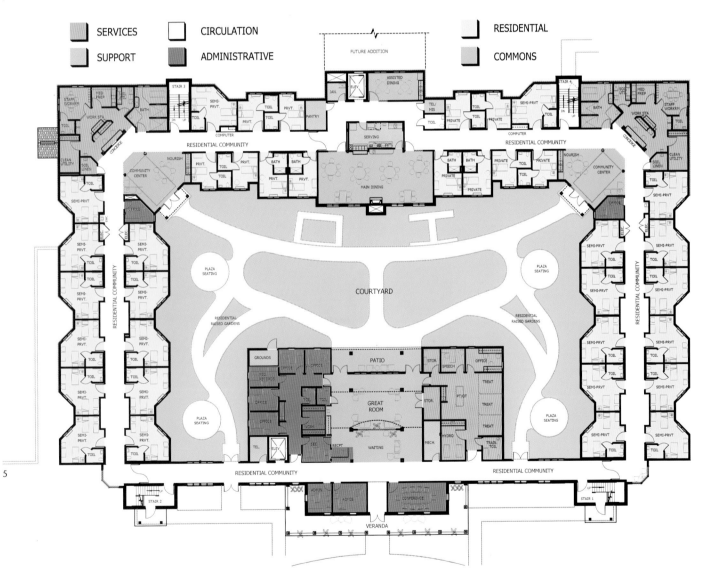

5

1 Cutaway view of great room
2 Detail of front south elevation
3 Front/south elevation
4 View from concierge to courtyard
5 Main floor plan

DESIGN FOR

SENIOR LIVING RESIDENCE
RESIDENCE

GING REVIEW

OUR LADY OF VICTORY CONVENT LEMONT, ILLINOIS

The Troyer Group, Inc.

Citation   *Addressing affordability as well as the specialized needs of its aging residents, this assisted living facility offers a respectful, spiritual residence with elegant simplicity. The design appropriately addresses both spiritual and secular requirements of the residents' care, blending them seamlessly without diminishing either.*

Architect's statement

The Franciscan Sisters of Chicago is a congregation of Catholic women with a mission focus that includes education, healthcare, social services and pastoral services for seniors, women, and children.

The Sisters' existing convent facility had become difficult and expensive to maintain and was too large for their needs. No air conditioning, worn finishes, and a facility with challenging circulation did not meet the needs of a fragile population. The goal was to create a high-quality and respectful living environment for the aging members to meet their healthcare needs and to also reflect their identity. They desired the design of a facility to be adaptable enough to allow it to serve as a laity-run assisted living facility at some time in the future.

The new convent provides a living and worship environment for 72 aging Sisters who require various levels of heathcare, and private sleeping and bathing arrangements. The new convent presents a warm and decidedly feminine character with interior colors and finishes that are soft, light, and cheerful. The Sisters desired an environment that was 'simple but nice' and this concept directed design decisions.

Site location	Suburban
Site area	20.3 acres/884,269 square feet
Capacity	72 assisted living units
Total project cost	Not available

1 *Main approach drive*
2 *Chapel exterior*
3 *Courtyard*
4 *Main entrance canopy*

Major design objectives

Create a care-giving, living environment for approximately 80 Sisters, most of whom are elderly

Provide independent congregate living in which the residents are able to care for themselves as the population continues to age

Consider that in the future the facility will be open to the laity. Consequently, strive to meet anticipated assisted living licensure standards

Create an environment that is comforting and familiar to the Sisters
While the residents provide their own care, there are two levels of care provided in the facility, with each having social areas for shared conversation and spiritual activities.

4

3

5

6

5 Section looking west
6 Views to courtyard and
   waterfall from second floor
   garden room bridge
7 Stained glass art panels
8 Stair detail
9 Two-story lobby

7

8

9

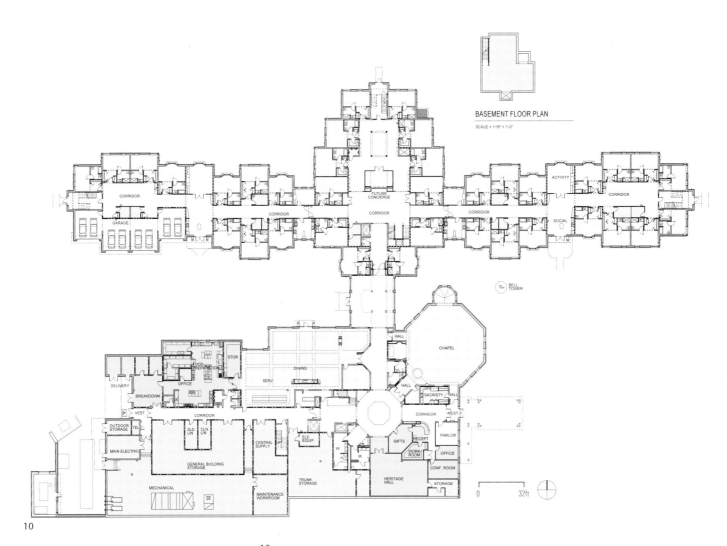

BASEMENT FLOOR PLAN

SCALE = 1/16" = 1'-0"

10

12

11

10   *First floor and basement floor plan*

11   *Garden room*

12   *Sacred Heart of Jesus chapel*

13   *Library area*

Photography: *Larry Morris; Henry Brothers, Co.;*
Pete Christie, Christie Photography

13

Casa Norte at Casa de Manana

La Jolla, California

SGPA Architecture and Planning / Associate architect: Fehlman LaBarre Architecture and Planning

Architect's statement

Casa Norte is an addition to Casa de Manana, a historic oceanfront retirement community in La Jolla, California. It is an independent living facility able to accommodate both ambulatory and non-ambulatory residents. The addition consists of 39 unique one- and two-bedroom living accommodations. Each unit contains a complete kitchen and laundry facility. Other facilities include an exercise room, craft room, beauty salon, computer room, conference room, meeting room, living room, mail/work room, and administrative offices.

Casa Norte harmonizes with the historical design and look of the existing Casa de Manana facility. This was accomplished through the integration of arches, recessed windows, pavers at exterior hardscape, clay tile and plaster that matched the texture, color, and finish of the existing facility. The restoration of the historic arcade and its incorporation into the new structure completed the aesthetic integration of new and old.

1 *Resident rooms on coast boulevard*
2 *Plaza and historic arcade looking southwest*
3 *Resident rooms and underground parking entry*
4 *Resident rooms looking east*

1

Site location	Urban
Site area	1.32 acres/57,324 square feet
Capacity	39 apartments
Total project cost	$10.8 M

2

3

4

Major design objectives and responses

Create a design that complements and includes the existing historical context

Restoration and relocation was completed by cutting the arcade into three sections and moving them intact to a temporary location. The three sections were then carefully placed back together and positioned in a site-specific location, integrating key building materials, proportions, and components of the existing historic structure.

Create unique, distinct, and functional living units

A variety of one- and two-bedroom units were designed so that most of them took advantage of ocean and courtyard views. Kitchens with full size appliances were integrated into each unit, and each has an exterior balcony with sliding glass French doors. The majority also have a front door that opens directly to the exterior.

Maximize utilization of site

A three-story structure was built by utilizing the existing terrain and locating the community areas on the lower level, which is partially below the adjacent grade. These rooms open onto light wells and landscaping to allow natural light and exterior access to these spaces.

Create a central gathering space for residents

The living room is adjacent to the front desk and has direct access to the existing historic structure. This access is used by residents to go to the dining room. The living room is further energized through large arched windows that look out onto the central courtyard.

Incorporate residents into the design and construction experience

Residents were involved during the design process and offered suggestions on the community functions that they would like incorporated as well as specific suggestions for individual units. Residents were also alerted to construction activities planned for the week. In addition to the meetings, periodic barbeques were planned for residents to socialize with the design and construction team.

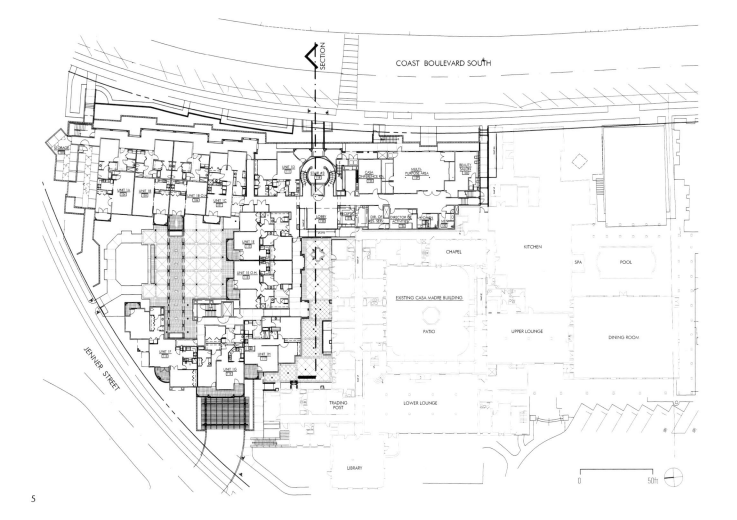

5 Site plan

6 Inca boy water feature and courtyard

7 Conference room

8 Typical resident room

9 Conference room

10 Lobby

11 Section

Photography: Erhard Pfeiffer

6

7

8

9

10

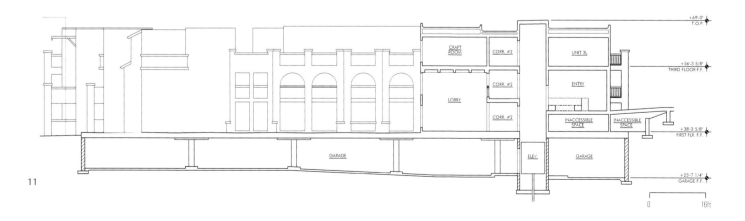

11

CHESTNUT SQUARE AT THE GLEN

GLENVIEW, ILLINOIS
Legat Architects, Inc.

Architect's statement

In 1998, the Glenview Village Board and the citizens of Glenview invited project teams to submit proposals for the acquisition of development parcels at the former Glenview Naval Air Station (GNAS). Approximately 714 of the total 1,121 acres are currently being redeveloped as residential neighborhoods, a mixed-use retail and entertainment complex, an 18-hole championship golf course and golf learning center, senior housing facilities, a business park, and private-sector recreation facilities.

Chestnut Square at The Glen won the competition for a 5-acre moderate- to high-density senior housing parcel, which is suited to meet the needs of seniors with a moderate income. The site is located in the center of the former GNAS and acts as a transition between the great park and relocated chapel across the street, adjacent residential neighborhoods, and the retail complex to the north. To respond to the Village of Glenview's character and community guidelines, Chestnut Square developed an identity through massing and material selections of the arts and crafts movement.

1

2

1 Exterior front
2 Site plan
3 Exterior
4 Garden room
5 Dining room
6 First floor plan

Chestnut Avenue

Patriot Boulevard

Site location	Suburban
Site area	7.7 acres/335,412 square feet
Capacity	164 units
Total project cost	$27.3 M

0   128ft

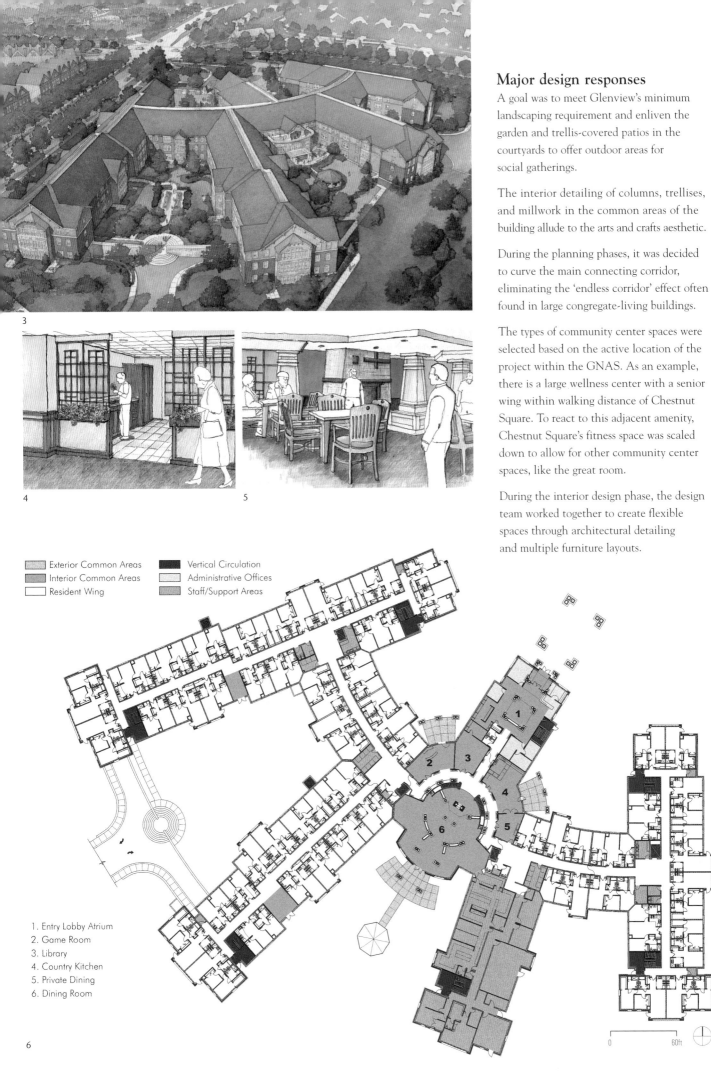

3

4   5

Major design responses

A goal was to meet Glenview's minimum landscaping requirement and enliven the garden and trellis-covered patios in the courtyards to offer outdoor areas for social gatherings.

The interior detailing of columns, trellises, and millwork in the common areas of the building allude to the arts and crafts aesthetic.

During the planning phases, it was decided to curve the main connecting corridor, eliminating the 'endless corridor' effect often found in large congregate-living buildings.

The types of community center spaces were selected based on the active location of the project within the GNAS. As an example, there is a large wellness center with a senior wing within walking distance of Chestnut Square. To react to this adjacent amenity, Chestnut Square's fitness space was scaled down to allow for other community center spaces, like the great room.

During the interior design phase, the design team worked together to create flexible spaces through architectural detailing and multiple furniture layouts.

Exterior Common Areas
Interior Common Areas
Resident Wing
Vertical Circulation
Administrative Offices
Staff/Support Areas

1. Entry Lobby Atrium
2. Game Room
3. Library
4. Country Kitchen
5. Private Dining
6. Dining Room

6

0   60ft

HOLY FAMILY VILLAGE

LEMONT, ILLINOIS

Nagle Hartray Danker Kagan McKay Penney Architects Ltd.

Architect's statement

The 17-acre Holy Family Village development is phase 1 of a 237-acre masterplan for religious and senior housing, serving the aging Catholic population of Lemont and its neighboring communities, while also providing housing for retired archdiocesan priests from parishes of Chicago's south side.

The 99-bed skilled nursing residence is designed as a replacement facility for the original 1950's Holy Family Villa, owned and operated by the Catholic Charities of Chicago. Drawing from European models, the 'neighborhood' concept was implemented to reduce the scale of the facility while enhancing the homelike atmosphere for the residents.

The Bishop Timothy J. Lyne residence is the first of its kind in the archdiocese. It is designed to house 18 priests in a communal setting with a common dining room, community rooms, exercise room, and chapel.

1

Site location	Rural
Site area	17 acres/740,520 square feet
Capacity	18 assisted living units;
	99 skilled nursing care beds
Total project cost	$15.9 M

2

3

4

6

5

Major design objectives and responses

Incorporate contemporary ideas about nursing home design, while creating a homelike setting with a residential character

The 'neighborhood' concept was implemented with a central nursing station/gazebo serving as the activity hub for the residents and nursing staff. L-shaped resident unit types were designed to avoid side-by-side bed arrangements. The exterior was designed with brick veneer, gabled and hipped roofs, balconies, and limestone trim to create a residential character.

Design a residence for 18 retired priests based on an assisted living prototype with the same amenities as a typical parish rectory

A one-bedroom unit type was developed with walk-in closets, roll-in showers, kitchenettes, and a large living/dining space. A chapel and communal gathering/dining spaces were also provided off the main entrance. Parking garages were designed and sited to complement the residential character of the development.

Provide a central power plant for both buildings and an enclosed pedestrian connection for easy access

A central mechanical/power plant for the new development was integrated into the roof and basement of the Lyne Residence. A tunnel connection was provided for transporting food and laundry to/from both buildings, while also serving as a means for routing all mechanical, electrical, and plumbing lines from the power plant to the nursing residence.

Develop a site plan that responds to the natural character of the rural surroundings

A meandering driveway and detention pond were designed to enhance the experience of arrival to the development. The buildings are sited at slight angles to each other to form an inviting entry court with the nursing home chapel and tower anchoring the development. The wings of the nursing residence form courtyards with open views toward the natural surroundings, and a pedestrian walkway was designed to create a path around both buildings.

1   Bishop Lyne residence, north entrance
2   Skilled nursing residence, nurse's station
3   Exterior of Bishop Lyne and skilled nursing residence
4   Bishop Lyne residence, chapel
5   Skilled nursing residence, chapel
6   Bishop Lyne residence, dining room

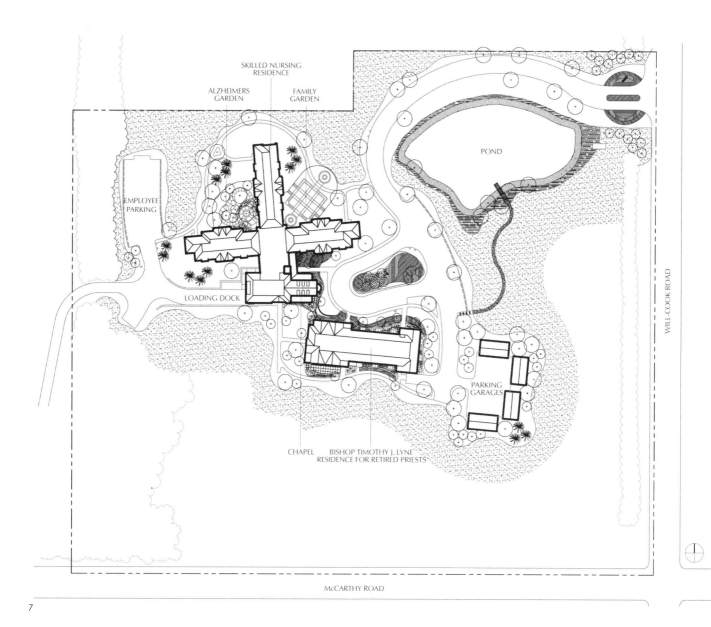

SKILLED NURSING
RESIDENCE

ALZHEIMERS   FAMILY
GARDEN   GARDEN

POND

EMPLOYEE
PARKING

LOADING DOCK

PARKING
GARAGES

CHAPEL   BISHOP TIMOTHY J. LYNE
RESIDENCE FOR RETIRED PRIESTS

WILL-COOK ROAD

McCARTHY ROAD

7

8

7   Site plan

8   Skilled nursing residence, resident room

9   Skilled nursing residence, east elevation
    and section

10 Bishop Lyne residence, first floor plan

11 Bishop Lyne residence, resident suite

12 Bishop Lyne residence, living room

Photography: Bruce Van Inwegen

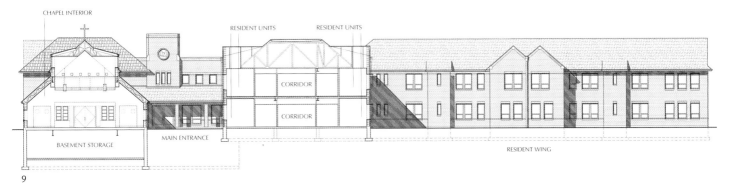

CHAPEL INTERIOR

RESIDENT UNITS   RESIDENT UNITS

CORRIDOR

CORRIDOR

BASEMENT STORAGE

MAIN ENTRANCE

RESIDENT WING

9

MAIN
ENTRANCE

CHAPEL

OFFICE

LOUNGE

REC.

LOBBY

TYPICAL
RESIDENT
SUITE

DINING
ROOM

COMMUNITY
ROOM

0   20ft

10

11

12

LA VIDA REAL

RANCHO SAN DIEGO, CALIFORNIA
Mithun

Architect's statement

This independent and assisted living community enhances the quality of lifestyle available for seniors by creating a hospitality-oriented residential environment that fosters independence, choice, dignity, and privacy tailored to a Southern Californian environment.

Using a Spanish Colonial style, the community expresses the metaphor of a Spanish hill-town where the main entry courtyard anchors the town center, with its civic and hospitality-inspired spaces as the main common areas. Residential wings branch from this central courtyard and take on a less formal growth by accretion image, characteristic of buildings developed over time. Façade treatments of resident wings were purposely varied in order to avoid the repeated multifamily look.

The building expresses a clear sense of arrival and an intuitive pedestrian circulation system. A strong hierarchy of circulation links and nodes defines the public spaces, as well as the semi-public and private spaces. These circulation spaces transcend mere hallways or corridors and become galleries, loggias, and edges of prominent common spaces, oriented toward vistas of the various landscaped outdoor courtyards. The classic interweaving of indoor to outdoor space is what makes this project special.

Site location	Suburban
Site area	11 acres
Capacity	210 apartments; 98 assisted living units; 14 special care for persons with dementia
Total project cost	$52 M

3

4

Major design objectives and responses

Design in a Spanish Colonial style
Appropriate to Southern California, the architectural vernacular was selected based on the zoning criteria and design standards of the municipality, with a slight variation in that it evokes a metaphor of a Spanish hill-town

Provide an intuitive sense of orientation when arriving and moving about the community
The circulation spaces do not appear as mere hallways or corridors—they become galleries, loggias, and edges of the prominent common spaces that are oriented to vistas of the landscaped outdoor courtyards; a classic interweaving of indoor to outdoor space.

Create a high-quality environment within a defined budget
A distinct hierarchy of interior details and finishes was judiciously created, with the highest levels in the common spaces and moderate levels in the units.

Landscape that supports the spirit of the new community
The perimeter landscaping of the project suggests a blending of landscape continuity with the neighborhood, while announcing something above the norm and unique for this project. Special consideration was given to utilizing drought-resistant plant materials and maintaining indigenous species. The project's main entry is clearly defined from the street, with its elegant drop-off area, outdoor entry rotunda, enriched paving, trellises, pots, and colorful plant materials.

The courtyards form the heart of the project. Each individual courtyard exhibits a unique landscape character, with distinct paving, trellises, pavilions, and plant material selections that are complementary to the architecture. Most of these courtyards extend from the project perimeter deep into the building mass where they provide natural light and air, as well as important outdoor space adjacent to the common spaces and varied residential neighborhoods.

1 Approach to entry from auto court
2 Entry courtyard with pool courtyard beyond
3 Pool
4 Residential courtyard

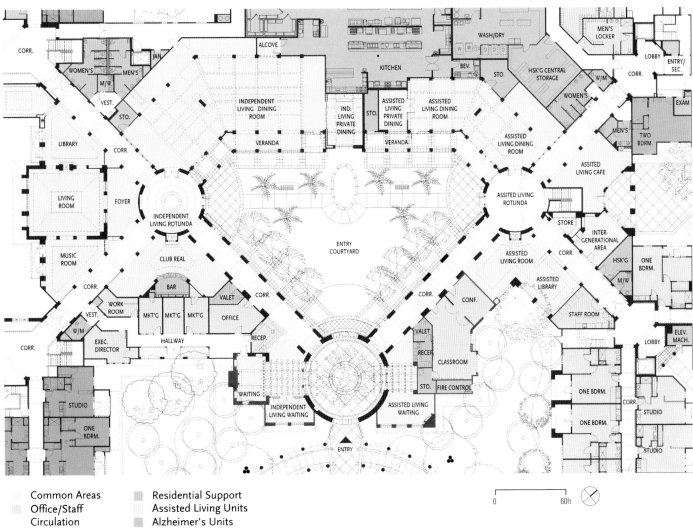

Common Areas
Office/Staff
Circulation
Service

Residential Support
Assisted Living Units
Alzheimer's Units
Independent Living Units

0   60ft

6

7   8

Opposite   *Entry lobby*

6   *Level one floor/site plan*

7   *Lounge adjacent to dining room*

8   *Library with living room beyond*

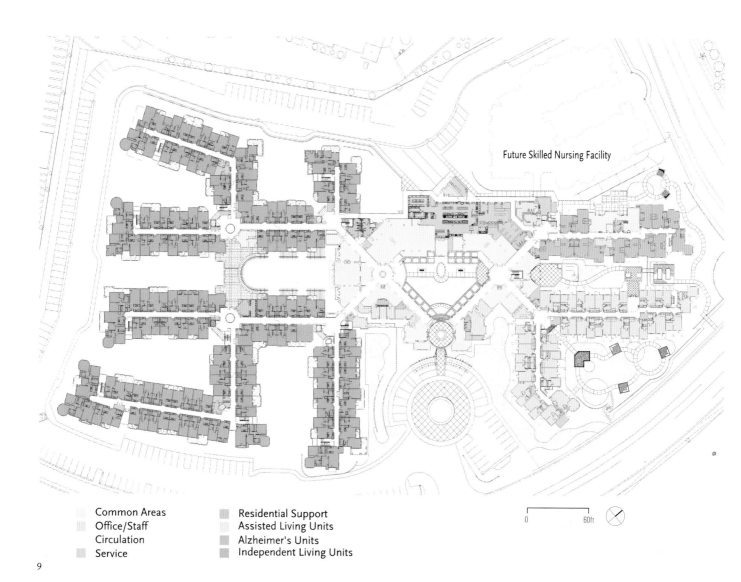

Future Skilled Nursing Facility

░ Common Areas
▓ Office/Staff
  Circulation
▓ Service

▓ Residential Support
░ Assisted Living Units
▓ Alzheimer's Units
▓ Independent Living Units

0   60ft

9

9   *Level two floor/site plan*
10 *Studio alcove unit*
11 *Independent living room*
12 *Dining room*

Photography:

Architectural Photography, Inc.

10

11

12

DESIGN FOR

PACE at St. Cecilia

New Orleans, Louisiana

Blitch/Knevel Architects, Inc.

Citation

In this conversion of a local architectural icon from spiritual use to the service of neighborhood seniors, the architect and client took a contemporary approach to sensitively reusing the space. The resulting facility provides for the physical, social, and emotional needs of residents in a way that respects the setting and enhances the neighborhood. This project exemplifies the concept of designing model care for the elderly while maintaining the built context as well as the social fabric of the community.

Architect's statement

PACE at St. Cecilia is the first program of its kind in Louisiana, converting a historic Gothic church and rectory (closed in 2001) into a PACE program (Program of All-Inclusive Care for the Elderly) for 120 participants from the local region. The main sanctuary will serve as multifunctional activity space, to preserve its historic character, and the rectory will be converted to a clinical wing. Minor new additions will provide a covered drop-off for vans transporting participants to and from the program, and a new therapy gym with garden views. The enclosed court between the activity spaces and clinic will become an accessible therapy garden. PACE participants are picked up at home every morning and brought to St. Cecilia for meals, activities, physical and social therapy, and clinical visits to doctors, dentists, and specialists. PACE at St. Cecilia will return the church to its neighborhood, while serving its aging population and prolonging independence.

1

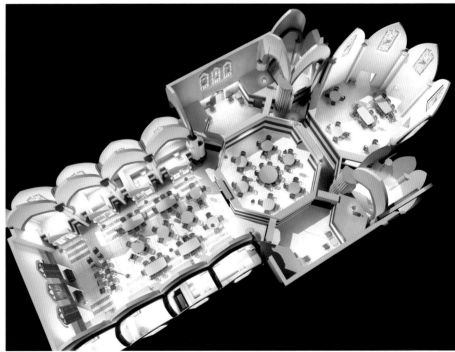

2

Size of project	82,000 square feet
People served by project	150 participants
Total project cost	$2.9 M
Cost	$110 per square foot

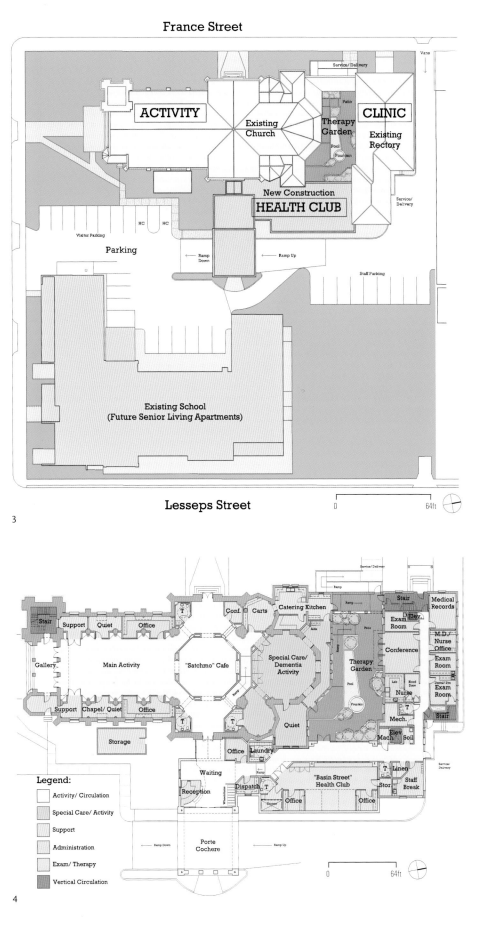

France Street

ACTIVITY

Existing Church

Therapy Garden

CLINIC

Existing Rectory

Pool
Fountain

Service/ Delivery

Vans

New Construction
HEALTH CLUB

Service/ Delivery

Visitor Parking

HC   HC

Parking

Ramp Down

Ramp Up

Staff Parking

Existing School
(Future Senior Living Apartments)

Lesseps Street

0   64ft

3

Stair
Support
Quiet
Office

Conf.   Carts
Catering Kitchen

Service/ Delivery
Ramp

Stair

Medical Records

Exam Room   Elev.

M.D./ Nurse Office

Gallery

Main Activity

"Satchmo" Cafe

Special Care/ Dementia Activity

Therapy Garden

Conference

Exam Room

Lab   Flood Door

Dental/ Eye Exam Room

Nurse

Support
Chapel/ Quiet
Office

Pool
Fountain

Mech.

Stair

Storage

Quiet

Elev Mach.

Soil

Office   Laundry

Waiting

Office

Ramp

"Basin Street" Health Club

Linen

Stor

Staff Break

Reception

Dispatch

Shower

Office

Office

Legend:

Activity/ Circulation

Special Care/ Activity

Support

Administration

Exam/ Therapy

Vertical Circulation

Ramp Down

Porte Cochere

Ramp Up

Service/ Delivery

0   64ft

4

1 Interior
2 Aerial view of interior
3 Site plan
4 First floor plan

Special features

The design team and sponsors visited numerous PACE facilities to see the program in action, and determined that the church complex could be successfully adapted to house the program.

To preserve the original appearance of the church interior, it will be divided into three main activity areas. The design will respect the Gothic context of its interior, with custom-designed wall finishes (banding), lighting fixtures, and floor patterns. Offices and toilets will be recessed into the original side aisles of the main sanctuary. Altars, statuary, and pews were removed in the decommissioning of the church, while the stained glass remained due to its historical significance.

The original church sanctuary offers direct access to the therapy garden. Quiet areas are provided for participants when needed, and the space is flexible in design to allow varied activities.

The entrance to PACE at St. Cecilia begins with a glass atrium connection to the original exterior door, with the stained glass side aisle windows visible above. While respecting the historic fabric, this orients participants to their location. Throughout the facility, participants can view the exterior through large window walls.

Nicarry Meetinghouse

New Oxford, Pennsylvania

Reese, Lower, Patrick & Scott, Ltd.

Architect's statement

Light, simplicity, and a strong connection to outdoor gardens shaped the design of this on-campus, multipurpose worship space for a retirement community that is home to nearly 900 people. Owned by The Brethren Home Community, it provides spiritual nourishment for campus residents and members of the surrounding community at large.

The new meetinghouse, which was part of a larger project including skilled care facility renovations and additions, and construction of a new 85,000-square-foot apartment building, serves as a spiritual, social, and physical focal point for the campus. The building links with existing nursing care wings to form a new landscaped courtyard, creating a sense of place at the hub of the formerly disordered arrangement of multiple building additions. Newly renovated therapy facilities line the garden courtyard, taking advantage of generous natural light and access to the outdoors in fair weather.

1

2

3

4

Size of project	14,500 square feet
People served by project	900
Total project cost	$1.8 M
Cost	$125 per square foot

1 Exterior courtyard
2 Main entrance and garden
3 Courtyard and connection to skilled care dining
4 Interior sanctuary
5 Section
6 Floor plan
Photography: Larry Lefever Photography

Special features

The meetinghouse design reflects the congregation's desire for a simple gathering place with minimal use of religious symbolism or ornamentation. While emphasizing the religious character of the building, the design provides flexibility to serve as a multipurpose worship and meeting facility with a seating capacity of 380. It can be divided into three smaller meeting rooms, all with clerestory lighting on both the north and south sides to accommodate fine art programs, in-service functions, and meetings in addition to the primary religious functions. A glass wall at the east end of the meetinghouse provides views of the courtyard, which extends the apparent volume of the meetinghouse and serves as an outdoor gathering space.
A meditation room and pastoral office adjoin the main assembly room.

5

0   5ft

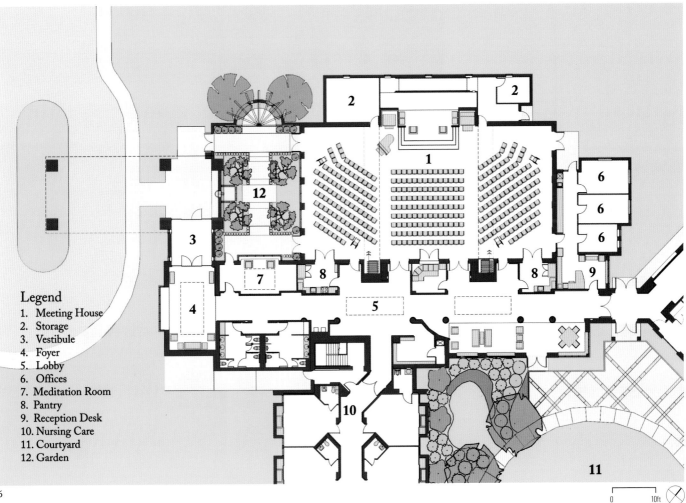

Legend
1. Meeting House
2. Storage
3. Vestibule
4. Foyer
5. Lobby
6. Offices
7. Meditation Room
8. Pantry
9. Reception Desk
10. Nursing Care
11. Courtyard
12. Garden

6

0   10ft

WILLOW VALLEY CULTURAL CENTER

LANCASTER, PENNSYLVANIA

Bernardon Haber Holloway Architects PC

Architect's statement

This is a two-story stand-alone building designed on the side of a hill to appear as a single-story facility. This low profile design strategy helped to address the site issue of the close proximity of a residential neighborhood and to help offset the building height needed to accommodate the interior uses. The two levels of the building are very different and are accessed by their own separate entrances.

The facility is the result of 20 years of experience in serving the needs of seniors. It has successfully created a new and exciting environment where the residents can be participants or patrons of the arts, express themselves, or simply relax in good company. The traditional senior center is a place of the past; today, we provide a cultural center to nurture and celebrate the convergence of mind, body, and spirit.

1

2

Size of project	82,000 square feet
People served by project	2,100
Total project cost	$9.1 M
Cost	$111 per square foot

3

Special features

The lower or informal level provides a full range of activities and amenities that help promote a healthy and active body, and an energized spirit. Areas include:

- 15,000-square-foot natatorium with three pools
- 8,000-square-foot fitness center with perimeter jogging track and complete computerized record-keeping capabilities
- Vitality Café and lounge that serves health-conscious foods and snacks
- 2,500-square-foot therapy suite with a discrete area for rehabilitation and strength development
- 1,500-square-foot day spa with massage, wrap, skin care, and manicure/pedicure services
- multipurpose room for model train hobbyists
- 1,200-square-foot aerobics room
- 2,500 square feet of locker room areas with separate facilities for both residents and team members

In contrast, the upper or formal level is very traditional. This includes:

- 500-seat recital hall equipped with state-of-the-art sound, lighting, rigging, and video systems
- 240-person banquet room
- 1,600 square feet of meeting/conference rooms
- classrooms for adult education programs
- art studio
- business center
- 3,000-square-foot grand lobby entrance and concourse area
- 30-foot-wide gallery that extends the length of the building, used for the display of resident artwork

This formal level helps to stimulate the mind and spirit, offering residents a broad range of cultural experiences through music, art, and literature. The interiors are elegant with rich mahogany trim throughout. The large expanses of space are instrumental in offering the residents areas in which to interact and socialize.

1   *Lower level entrance*
2   *Upper level entrance*
3   *Lower level reception area*
4&5   *Vitality Café*

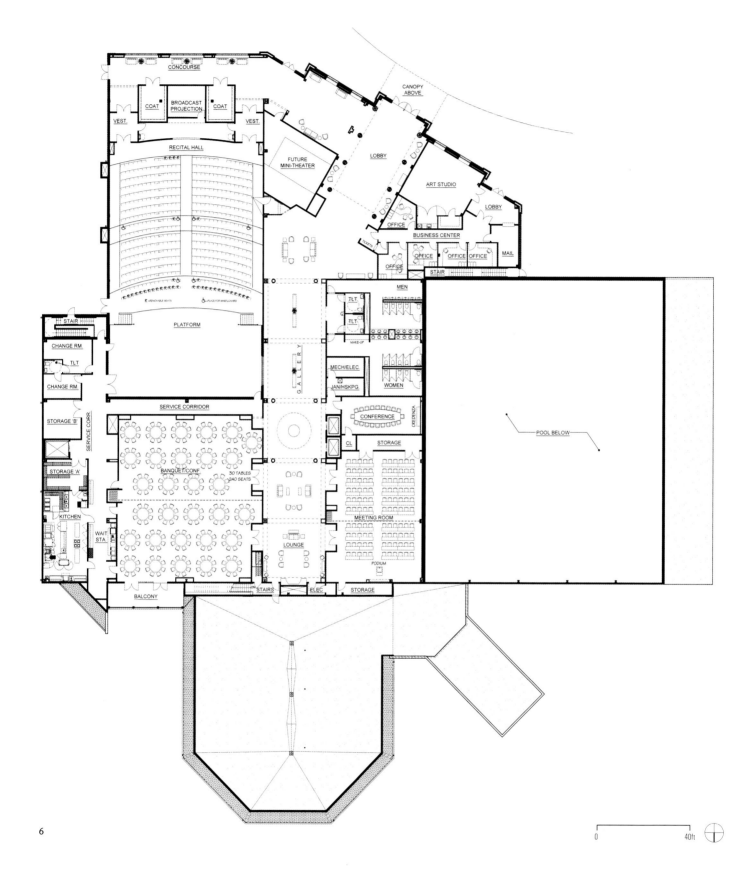

CONCOURSE

COAT BROADCAST PROJECTION COAT

VEST. VEST.

CANOPY ABOVE

RECITAL HALL

FUTURE MINI-THEATER

LOBBY

ART STUDIO

LOBBY

OFFICE

BUSINESS CENTER

OFFICE OFFICE OFFICE MAIL

OFFICE

TICKETS

STAIR

MEN

R-REMOVABLE SEATS ⚬-PLACE FOR WHEELCHAIRS

STAIR

TLT
TLT
MAKE-UP

PLATFORM

CHANGE RM.

TLT

CHANGE RM.

MECH/ELEC.

JAN/HSKPG.

WOMEN

G A L L E R Y

STORAGE 'B'

CONFERENCE

CREDENZA

SERVICE CORRIDOR

CL

STORAGE

POOL BELOW

STORAGE 'A'

BANQUET/CONF.

30 TABLES
240 SEATS

SERVICE CORR.

KITCHEN

WAIT STA.

LOUNGE

MEETING ROOM

PODIUM

BALCONY

STAIRS ELEC STORAGE

6

0   40ft

6 *Upper level floor plan*
7 *Upper level lobby*
8 *Upper level banquet room*
9 *Upper level lounge*
Photography: *Tim Schoon Photographer*

7

8

9

DESIGN FOR

RESEARCH PROJECT
GING REVIEW

Sunset Village Café

Jenison, Michigan

Dorsky Hodgson + Partners, Inc.

Architect's statement

The Café/Soda Shop is the focal point of a 54-unit addition to an existing campus. Specific design directives for the uniqueness of the Café are:

- Use the design of the Café to create a resident-oriented social space to link new and existing buildings
- Locate the Café adjacent to the new entry to create an enlivening space
- Provide multiple seating areas for formal and informal dining, coffee breaks, tea time, and snacks
- Provide garden views and natural light
- Allow for open circulation, easy accessibility, visual connections throughout the Café, yet provide clear space delineations for the various seating areas to allow for intimate spaces and large groups sitting together
- Orient a circulation spine past the Café that visually directs people to the reception area in the existing building
- Incorporate all of the client's must-have features that create the ambiance of a café/soda shop
- A behavior mapping study was conducted from 7:30 am until 9:00 pm. Every 30 minutes a snapshot was taken of the activities occurring in the space, recording the location of users, and what they were doing. Residents, staff, and visitors were also interviewed.

1

2   3

1   Entry canopy
2   Entry lobby
3&6   Café
4   Garden dining
5   First floor plan

Photography: carr cialdella photography

Size of project	Café/9,745 square feet + 54-unit congregate/60,007 square feet
People served by project	Unlimited
Total project cost	$5.95 M (Café and congregate)
Cost	$85.32 per square foot

4

Some observations about the space

A space for the multiple choice generation

Initially the campus had two formal dining rooms and a self-serve café with limited food items.

Residents now have multiple choices of dining venues and menu options. They can select from standard meals available in the dining rooms, or order from the Café/Soda Shop menu, choosing to dine in the formal dining area, have their meal in the Soda Shop, eat at the counter, or order take-out.

A social place that appeals to all generations

The old-fashioned café has universal appeal since it provides a comfortable place for residents to entertain guests and family members. The staff enjoy the Soda Shop, too. They were frequently found ordering take-out or enjoying coffee and soda. As many as nine family members were observed visiting a single resident at one time. Children were often found in the Soda Shop and two teenage boys were visiting their grandparents during lunch. Clearly, the Soda Shop is a place to show-off grandchildren and great grandchildren. One resident said, her great granddaughter tells her mother, 'I want to go visit grandmother with the good french fries.'

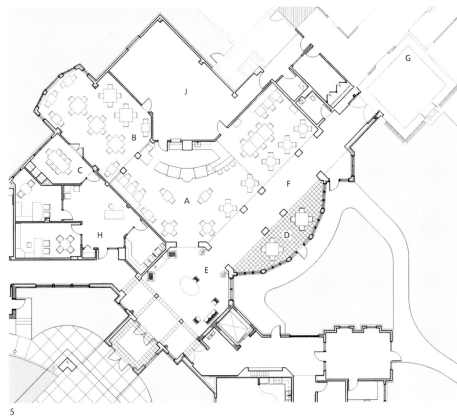

5

6

Key:
A   Café
B   Formal dining
C   Conference room
D   Garden dining
E   Main entry lobby
F   Grand hall
G   Reception
H   Marketing
J   Kitchen

DESIGN FOR

PROJECT DATA
GING REVIEW

ABRAMSON CENTER FOR JEWISH LIFE

Status of project: Completed March 2002
Facility administrator: Frank Podietz
Owner: Abramson Center for Jewish Life
Architect: EwingCole
Associated architect: Nelson-Tremain Partnership, P.A.
Interior designer: Elizabeth Brawley, ASID
Landscape architect: Carter Van Dyke Associates, Inc.
Structural engineer: EwingCole
Mechanical engineer: EwingCole
Electrical engineer: EwingCole
Civil engineer: Charles E. Shoemaker, Inc.
Contractor: R.M. Shoemaker Company
Mosaic artist: Jonathan Mandel

PROJECT AREAS

Project element	included in this project				
	units, beds, or clients	new GSF	renovated GSF	total gross area	total on site or served by project
Senior living/assisted living/personal care (units)	48	47,488			48
Skilled nursing care (beds)	324	105,300		324	
Common social areas (people)		43,735			
Kitchen (daily meals served)		9,300			
Elder day care (clients)	20	3,500			20
Children's day care (clients)	60	3,500			60
Retail space (shops/restaurants, etc)		2,150			
Fitness/rehab/wellness (daily visits)		7,180			

ASSISTED LIVING FACILITIES
General social/residential assisted living models

Project element	new construction		
	no. units	typical size	
Studio units	24	338	
One bedroom units	24	518	
Total (all units)	48	20,544	
Residents' social areas (lounges, dining, and recreation spaces)		10,520	
Administrative, public, and ancillary support services		1,440	
Service, maintenance, and mechanical areas		3,180	
Total gross area		47,488	

NURSING FACILITIES
Skilled nursing facilities

Project element	new construction		
	no. beds	typical room size	
Residents in one-bed/single rooms	324	325	
No. of residents			
rooms	324		
beds	324	105,300	
Social areas (lounges, dining, and recreation spaces)		43,800	
Medical, healthcare, therapies, and activities spaces		7,180	
Administrative, public, and ancillary support services		30,800	
Service, maintenance, and mechanical areas		28,000	
Total gross area		342,362	

OTHER FACILITIES

Project element	new construction		
	no. size	size	
Adult day care	20	3,500	
Child day care	60	3,500	
Total		7,000	
Total gross area		7,000	

CONSTRUCTION COSTS

The following information is based on actual costs
Final construction cost as of June 2002
Financing sources: taxable bond offering

Building costs
Total building costs $62.1 M
Site costs
Total site costs $4 M
Total project costs   **$70.7 M**

AVALON SQUARE

Status of project: August 2003
Facility administrator: David Fulcher
Owner: Presbyterian Homes of Wisconsin
Architect: KKE Architects, Inc.
Interior designer: Encompass Interiors
Structural engineer: Pierce Engineers, Inc.
Mechanical engineer: Design / Build
Electrical engineer: Design / Build
Civil engineer: Jahnke & Jahnke Assoc., Inc.
Contractor: The Jansen Group, Incorporated

PROJECT AREAS

Project element	included in this project				
	units, beds, or clients	new GSF	renovated GSF	total gross area	total on site or served by project
Apartments (units)	68	79,046		79,046	79,046
Senior living/assisted living/personal care (units)	52	22,036	20,526	42,562	42,562
Special care for persons with dementia	27	11,018	6,842	17,860	17,860
Common social areas (people)		22,000	8,166	30,166	30,166
Kitchen (daily meals served)	215	504	2,254	2,758	2,758
Elder outreach (clients) (home health)	120	600		600	600
Retail space (shops/restaurants, etc)		12,606		12,606	12,606
Fitness/rehab/wellness (daily visits)	35	3,212		3,212	3,212
Total		151,022	37,788		188,810

RESIDENTIAL FACILITIES

Project element	cottages		apartments	
		no.	typical size GSF	size range GSF
One bedroom units	24			675–807
One bedroom/den units	27			929–1,091
Two bedroom units	15			1,157–1,216
Two bedroom plus den units	2			1,700
Total (all units)	68			66,565
Residents' social areas (lounges, dining, and recreation spaces)		town center	27,560	
Medical/health/fitness and activities areas		town center	3,776	
Administrative, public, and ancillary support service areas		town center	425	
Service, maintenance, and mechanical areas		town center	3,580	
Total gross area			105,731	

ASSISTED LIVING FACILITIES
General social/residential assisted living models

Project element	new construction		renovations	
	no. units	typical size GSF	no. units	typical size GSF
Studio units			27	415
One bedroom units	20	697	3	680
Two bedroom units	2	1,027		
Total (all units)	52	15,994		13,245
Residents' social areas (lounges, dining, and recreation spaces)		on floors		785
Administrative, public, and ancillary support services		on floors		880
Total gross area		on floors		30,904

Dementia-specific assisted living models

Project element	new construction		renovations	
	no. units	typical size GSF	no. units	typical size GSF
Studio units	14	428	12	300
One bedroom units	1	575		
Total (all units)	27	6,567		3,600
Residents' social areas (lounges, dining, and recreation spaces)		on floor		2,081
Administrative, public, and ancillary support services		on floor		455
Total gross area				12,703

OTHER FACILITIES

Project element	new construction	
	no.	size
Wellness/fitness center	1	3,212

CONSTRUCTION COSTS

The following information is based on actual costs
Final construction cost as of August 2003
Financing sources: non-taxable bond offering

Building costs
Total building costs — $16 M
Site costs
Total site costs — $1.1 M
Total project costs — **$22.85 M**

Brewster Village

Status of project: Completed September 2001
Facility administrator: David Rothmann
Owner: Outagamie County
Architect: Horty Elving
Interior designer: Horty Elving
Landscape architect: Close Landscape Architecture
Structural engineer: Horty Elving
Mechanical engineer: Horty Elving
Electrical engineer: Bussell Companies
Civil engineer: Horty Elving
Contractor: Oscar J Boldt Construction

PROJECT AREAS

Project element	included in this project				
	units, beds, or clients	new GSF	renovated GSF	total gross area	total on site or served by project
Skilled nursing care (beds)	204				204

NURSING FACILITIES
Skilled nursing facilities

Project element	new construction	
	no. beds	typical room size
Residents in one-bed/single rooms	204	273 (with toilet room)

CONSTRUCTION COSTS

The following information is based on actual costs

Building costs
Total building costs — $21 M
Total project costs — **$24.1 M**

Brigham House

Status of project: Completed October 2002
Facility administrator: Tom Burns
Owner: The Baran Companies
Architect: The Architectural Team, Inc.
Interior designer: Karin Mahious and Paloma Ferreira
Landscape architect: A.J. Tomasi Landscape Architects
Structural engineer: Charles Chaloff Consulting Engineers, Inc.
Mechanical engineer: Q&W Associates
Electrical engineer: Q&W Associates
Civil engineer: SITEC, Inc.

PROJECT AREAS

Project element	included in this project				
	units, beds, or clients	new GSF	renovated GSF	total gross area	total on site or served by project
Senior living/assisted living/personal care (units)	60			+- 38,000	60
Common social areas (people)	7				7
Kitchen (daily meals served)			1,500	1,500	3 meals
Retail space (shops/ restaurants, etc)	1				1
Fitness/rehab/wellness (daily visits)	1	1,100			1

ASSISTED LIVING FACILITIES
General social/residential assisted living models

Project element	new construction		renovations	
	no. units	typical size GSF	no. units	typical size
Studio units	60	400		
Total (all units)	60			
Residents' social areas (lounges, dining, and recreation spaces)				1,200
Medical, healthcare, therapies, and activities spaces				1,200
Administrative, public, and ancillary support services				1,500
Service, maintenance, and mechanical areas				1,250
Total gross area				60,000

CONSTRUCTION COSTS

The following information is based on actual costs
Total project costs — **$7.5 M**

Brooksby Village, Phase 1

Status of project: Phase one completed September 2003; Estimated
completion date for entire campus September 2006
Facility administrator: Scott Hayward
Owner: Erickson Retirement Communities
Architect: Steffian Bradley Architects
Interior designer: Steffian Bradley Architects
Landscape architect: Carol R. Johnson Associates, Inc.
Structural engineer: D.M Berg Consultants
Mechanical engineer: Zade Company, Inc.
Electrical engineer: Zade Company, Inc.
Civil engineer: Beals & Thomas
Contractor: Beaver Builders Ltd.

PROJECT AREAS

Project element	included in this project				
	units, beds, or clients	new GSF	renovated GSF	total gross area	total on site or served by project
Continuing-care retirement communities	1,350 units	1,293,654		1,293,654	1,293,654
Common social areas (people)					1,200
Kitchen (daily meals served)					1,090
Retail space (shops, restaurants, etc)					2,300 people
Fitness/rehab/wellness (daily visits)					200
Pool(s) and related areas (users)					150

RESIDENTIAL FACILITIES

Project element	apartments		
	no.	typical size GSF	size range GSF
Studio units	25	512	362–600
One bedroom units	498	701	701–851
Two bedroom units	115	948	948–1,025
Two bedroom plus den units	712	1,066	909–1,478
Total (all units)		1,350	1,293,654
Residents' social areas (lounges, dining, and recreation spaces)		52,079	
Medical/health/fitness and activities areas		49,438	
Administrative, public, and ancillary support service areas		36,233	
Service, maintenance, and mechanical areas		44,839	
Total gross area		1,476,243	

CONSTRUCTION COSTS

Total project costs   Owner withheld

Carleton–Willard Village Nursing & Retirement Center

Status of project: Completed June 2002
Facility administrator: Barbara A. Doyle
Owner: Carleton–Willard Village, Inc
Architect: Tsomides Associates Architects Planners/TAAP
Interior designer: Woodman Design Group
Landscape architect: Carol R. Johnson Associates
Structural engineer: Foley & Buhl Engineering, Inc.
Mechanical engineer: Zade Company, Inc.
Electrical engineer: Zade Company, Inc.
Civil engineer: Commonwealth Engineering, Inc.
Contractor: Linbeck/Kennedy & Rossi, Inc.

PROJECT AREAS

Project element	included in this project				
	units, beds, or clients	new GSF	renovated GSF	total gross area	total on site or served by project
Apartments (units)					67
Cottages/villas (units)					88
Senior living/assisted living/personal care (units)					69
Special care for persons with dementia	30				
Skilled nursing care (beds)	70	3,984	58,634	62,618	
Common social areas (people)					224
Fitness/rehab/wellness (daily visits)					80
Pool(s) and related areas (users)					90

NURSING FACILITIES

Project element	new construction		renovations	
		typical room size GSF	no. beds	typical room size GSF
Residents in one-bed/ single rooms			40	210
Residents in two-bed/ double rooms			60	360
No. of residents 100 rooms 70 beds		3,984	100	58,634
Social areas (lounges, dining, and recreation spaces)				7,301
Medical, healthcare, therapies, and activities spaces				2,125
Administrative, public, and ancillary support services				5,600
Service, maintenance, and mechanical areas				6,200
Total gross area				62,618

CONSTRUCTION COSTS

The following information is based on actual costs
Final construction cost as of June 2002
Financing sources: non-taxable bond offering

Building costs

Total building costs $9.2 M
Total project costs   **$10.7 M**

Carroll Campbell Place Alzheimer's Unit

Status of project: Completed April 2002
Facility administrator: Wayne Stowe
Owner: Lexington Medical Center Extended Care
Architect: Perkins & Will
Interior designer: Perkins & Will
Structural engineer: Sedki & Russ
Mechanical engineer: Lanna, Dunlap, Spriggs Consulting Engineers
Electrical engineer: Lanna, Dunlap, Spriggs Consulting Engineers
Civil engineer: Cox and Dinkins, Inc.
Contractor: McCrory Construction

PROJECT AREAS

Project element	included in this project				
	units, beds, or clients	new GSF	renovated GSF	total gross area	total on site or served by project
Skilled nursing care (beds) (All Alzheimer's beds)	36	25,413		25,413	25,413

NURSING FACILITIES
Skilled nursing facilities–all alzheimer's beds

Project element		new construction	
		no. beds	typical room size
Residents in one-bed/single rooms		36	278 incl toilet
No. of residents	36		
rooms	36		
beds	36		
Social areas (lounges, dining, and recreation spaces)			2,772
Medical, healthcare, therapies, and activities spaces			957
Administrative, public, and ancillary support services			3,440
Service, maintenance, and mechanical areas			455
Total gross area			25,413

CONSTRUCTION COSTS

The following information is based on actual costs
Final construction cost as of May 2002
Financing sources: cash paid by owner of hospital

Building costs
Total building costs .... $3.61 M
Site costs
Total site costs .... $1 M
Total project costs .... **$6 M**

Casa Norte at Casa de Manana

Status of project: Completed February 2001
Owner: Front Porch
Architect: SGPA Architecture and Planning
Associate architect: Fehlman LaBarre Architecture and Planning
Interior designer: Chow Design/Interspec
Landscape architect: Nowell + Associates
Structural engineer: Burkett + Wong
Mechanical engineer: LSW Engineers
Electrical engineer: LSW Engineers
Civil engineer: Stuart Engineering
Contractor: Sundt Construction

PROJECT AREAS

Project element	included in this project				
	units, beds, or clients	new GSF	renovated GSF	total gross area	total on site or served by project
Apartments (units)	39	57,324		57,324	201,679
Common social areas (people)	50				200
Fitness/rehab/wellness (daily visits)	20				

CONSTRUCTION COSTS

The following information is based on actual costs
Final construction cost as of November 2000

Building costs
Total building costs .... $9.7 M
Site costs
Total site costs .... $1 M
Total project costs .... **$10.8 M**

Chestnut Square at The Glen

Status of project: Completed October 2003
Owner: Bethany Methodist Corporation
Architect: Legat Architects, Inc.
Interior designer: Legat Architects, Inc.
Landscape architect: Ives Ryan Group
Structural engineer: Larson Engineering
Mechanical engineer: Melvin Cohen & Associates
Electrical engineer: Melvin Cohen & Associates
Civil engineer: Manhard Engineering
Contractor: Paul H. Schwendener, Inc.

PROJECT AREAS

Project element	included in this project				
	units, beds, or clients	new GSF	renovated GSF	total gross area	total on site or served by project
Apartments (units)	164	143,779		143,779	164
Common social areas (people)		21,068		21,068	
Kitchen (daily meals served)		1,053		1,053	

RESIDENTIAL FACILITIES

Project element	apartments		
	no.	typical size GSF	size range GSF
One bedroom units	45	600	540–695
Two bedroom units	115	900	795–1,170
Two bedroom plus den units	4	1390	1,390
Total (all units)		164	169,000
Residents' social areas (lounges, dining, and recreation spaces)		29,000	
Medical/health/fitness and activities areas		1100	
Administrative, public, and ancillary support service areas		42,000	
Service, maintenance, and mechanical areas		26,000	
Total gross area		267,100	

CONSTRUCTION COSTS

The following information is based on estimates
Financing sources: non-taxable bond offering of $33.5 M

Building costs
Total building costs $25.5 M
Site costs
Total site costs $1.7 M
Total project costs   **$ 27.3 M**

Collington Episcopal Life Care Community

Status of project: Completed August 2003
Facility administrator: Sally Erdman-Jones
Owner: Collington Episcopal Life Care Comunity
Architect: Perkins Eastman
Interior designer: Perkins Eastman
Landscape architect: Mahan Rykiel Associates, Inc.
Structural engineer: Atlantic Engineering Services
Mechanical engineer: Elwood S. Tower Corporation
Electrical engineer: Elwood S. Tower Corporation
Civil engineer: Greenhorne & O'Mara, Inc.
Contractor: Harkins Builders

PROJECT AREAS

Project element	included in this project				
	units, beds, or clients	new GSF	renovated GSF	total gross area	total on site or served by project
Apartments (units)	168	74,000	24,000	98,000	108,266
Cottages/villas (units)	208	54,000		54,000	254,000
Senior living/assisted living/personal care (units)	10		7,000	7,000	
Special care for persons with dementia	34	28,000		28,000	
Skilled nursing care (beds)	59		18,500	18,500	
Common social areas (people)	600				
Kitchen (daily meals served)	900				
Elder day care (clients)	8		1,000	1,000	
Retail space (shops/ restaurants, etc)	1		650	650	
Fitness/rehab/wellness (daily visits)	48	3,500	3,200	6,700	
Pool(s) and related areas (users)	36			5,120	

RESIDENTIAL FACILITIES
* Data does not include existing units

Project element	cottages			apartments		
	no.	typical size GSF	size range GSF	no.	typical size GSF	size range GSF
One bedroom units				10	900	810–940
Two bedroom units				19	1,100	1,050–1,150
Two bedroom plus den units	17	1,800	1,700–1,870	13	1,300	1,230–1,340
Three bedroom and larger units	11	2,135	2,150–2,120	0		
Total (all units)	28	54,000		52	98,000	
Residents' social areas (lounges, dining, and recreation spaces)					15,000	
Medical/health/fitness and activities areas					6,700	
Administrative, public, and ancillary support service areas					8,100	
Service, maintenance, and mechanical areas					8,000	
Total gross area					189,800	

ASSISTED LIVING FACILITIES
General social/residential assisted living models

Project element	renovations	
	no. units	typical size
One bedroom units	10	500
Total (all units)	10	5,250

Dementia-specific assisted living models

Project element	new construction		renovations	
	no. units	typical size	no. units	typical size
Shared units	2	465		
Single occupancy units	32	275		
Total (all units)	34	28,000		
Residents' social areas (lounges, dining, and recreation spaces)				6,000
Medical, healthcare, therapies, and activities spaces				1,500
Administrative, public, and ancillary support services				1,600
Service, maintenance, and mechanical areas				950
Total gross area				38,050

NURSING FACILITIES

Skilled nursing facilities

Project element	new construction		renovations	
	no. beds	typical room size	no. beds	typical room size
Residents in one-bed/ single rooms	12	290	39	300
Residents in two-bed/ double rooms			8	400
No. of residents rooms 54 beds 59	12	3,500	47	15,000
Social areas (lounges, dining, and recreation spaces)				5,200
Medical, healthcare, therapies, and activities spaces				800
Administrative, public, and ancillary support services				2,000
Total gross area				26,500

OTHER FACILITIES

Project element	new construction		renovations	
	no.	size GSF	no.	size GSF
Dining rooms	3	2,800	5	5,400
Auditorium			1	3,500
Library			1	2,000
Clocktower commons			1	1,800
Wellness center	1	3,500		
Interfaith chapel	1	1,300		
Classrooms	2	975		
Physical therapy			6	3,200
Barber/beauty			1	500
Creative arts			1	1,400
Flower room	1	450		
Social areas (lounges, dining, and recreation spaces)				15,000
Administrative, public, and ancillary support services				8,100
Service, maintenance, and mechanical areas				8,000
Total gross area				93,700

CONSTRUCTION COSTS

The following information is based on actual costs

Final construction cost as of August 2003

Financing sources: non-taxable bond offering through Maryland Health and Education Finance Authority

Building costs

Total building costs $32 M

Site costs

Total site costs $2 M

Total project costs   **$40 M**

COVENANT AT SOUTH HILLS

Status of project: Completed January 2003
Facility administrator: Marianne Hogg
Owner: B'nai B'rith
Developer: Greystone Communities
Architect: Cochran, Stephenson & Donkervoet, Inc.
Associate architect: Rothschild Architects
Interior designer: IDA
Landscape architect: Mahan Rykie Associates, Inc.
Structural engineer: Faisant Associates, Inc.
Mechanical engineer: SRBR, Inc
Electrical engineer: SRBR, Inc
Civil engineer: Civil & Environmental Consultants, Inc.
Contractor: LeCesse Construction Co.

PROJECT AREAS

Project element	included in this project				
	units, beds, or clients	new GSF	renovated GSF	total gross area	total on site or served by project
Apartments (units)	126	127,687		127,687	126
Cottages/villas (units)					
Senior living/assisted living/personal care (units)	48	20,736		20,736	48
Special care for persons with dementia	12	3,372		3,372	12
Skilled nursing care (beds)	46	7,444		7,444	46
Common social areas (people)		14,776		14,776	
Kitchen (daily meals served)	118	4,390		4,390	
Fitness/rehab/wellness (daily visits)		1,505		1,505	

RESIDENTIAL FACILITIES

Project element	apartments		
	no.	typical size GSF	size range GSF
One bedroom units	53	784	580–930
Two bedroom units	69	1,131	1,000–1,300
Two bedroom plus den units	4	1,445	1,445
Total (all units)	126	127,687	
Residents' social areas (lounges, dining, and recreation spaces)		5,128	
Medical/health/fitness and activities areas		2,234	
Administrative, public, and ancillary support service areas		42,184	
Service, maintenance, and mechanical areas		11,245	
Total gross area		188,478	

ASSISTED LIVING FACILITIES

General social/residential assisted living models

Project element	new construction		
	no. units	typical size	
Studio units	24	382	
One bedroom units	24	482	
Total (all units)	48	20,736	
Residents' social areas (lounges, dining, and recreation spaces)		3,685	
Medical, healthcare, therapies, and activities spaces		1,146	
Administrative, public, and ancillary support services		9,100	
Service, maintenance, and mechanical areas		520	
Total gross area		35,187	

CUTHBERTSON VILLAGE AT ALDERSGATE

Status of project: Completed May 2003
Faculty administrator: Reverend Raymond O. Hall
Owner: Aldersgate, A United Methodist Retirement Community
Architect: FreemanWhite, Inc.
Interior designer: FreemanWhite, Inc.
Landscape architect: Site Solutions
Structural engineer: King/Guinn Associates
Mechanical engineer: FreemanWhite, Inc.
Electrical engineer: FreemanWhite, Inc.
Civil engineer: Site Solutions
Contractor: Bovis Lend Lease

Dementia-specific assisted living models

Project element	new construction	
	no. units	typical size
Studio units	12	281
Total (all units)	12	3,372
Residents' social areas (lounges, dining, and recreation spaces)		780
Medical, healthcare, therapies, and activities spaces		284
Administrative, public, and ancillary support services		1,484
Service, maintenance, and mechanical areas		100
Total gross area		6,020

NURSING FACILITIES
Skilled nursing facilities

Project element	new construction	
	no. beds	typical room size
Residents in one-bed/ single rooms	34	272
Residents in two-bed/ double rooms	12	470
No. of residents 46 rooms 40 beds	46	7,444
Social areas (lounges, dining, and recreation spaces)		2,949
Medical, healthcare, therapies, and activities spaces		2,265
Administrative, public and ancillary support services		2,636
Service, maintenance, and mechanical areas		6,928
Total gross area		42,672*

*includes back of house for entire facility

CONSTRUCTION COSTS

The following information is based on actual costs

Final construction cost as of March 2003

Building costs		
Total building costs	$30.3 M	
Site costs		
Total site costs	$1.8 M	
Total project costs	**Not known**	

PROJECT AREAS

Project element	included in this project				
	units, beds, or clients	new GSF	renovated GSF	total gross area	total on site or served by project
Apartments (units)					197
Cottages/villas (units)					56
Senior living/assisted living/personal care (units)					27
Special care for persons with dementia	45	34,000		34,000	45
Skilled nursing care (beds)					104
Common social areas (people)					300
Kitchen (daily meals served)					700+
Fitness/rehab/wellness (daily visits)					65/day
Pool(s) and relates areas (users)					65/day
Alzheimers association resident services clinic adj. spec care					3,000 adj. SC

ASSISTED LIVING FACILITIES
Dementia-specific assisted living models

Project element	new unit construction		support + total construction	
	no. units	typical size GSF		typical size GSF
Studio units	45	270		
Total (all units)	45	11,700		
Residents' social areas for households (3 @ 1,850 SF)				5,500
Residents' social areas for town square, including café, cinema, spa, general store, pet shop, garden shop, town green, household porches				4,600
Administrative, public and ancillary support services				300
Medical health services area				750
Service, maintenance, and mechanical areas (1 mech rm./household + 400)				1,400
Total gross area				34,000

CONSTRUCTION COSTS

The following information is based on actual costs

Final construction cost as of May 2003

Financing sources: non-taxable bond offering

Total project costs	**$4 M**

EDGEMERE

Status of project: Completed March 2002
Facility administrator: Troy Hart, Greystone Communities, Inc.
Owner: Northwest Senior Housing Corp.
Architect: three
Interior designer: Bridget Bohacz and Associates
Landscape architect: Enviro Design
Structural engineer: LA Fuess and Partners
Mechanical engineer: CCRD Partners
Electrical engineer: CCRD Partners
Civil engineer: Huitt Zollars
Contractor identification: Andres Construction Services

PROJECT AREAS

Project element	included in this project				
	units, beds, or clients	new GSF	renovated GSF	total gross area	total on site or served by project
Apartments (units)	259	315,000		315,000	
Senior living/assisted living/ personal care (units)	60	35,000		35,000	
Special care for persons with dementia	45	14,200		14,200	
Skilled nursing care (beds)	66	14,100		14,100	
Common social areas (people)		50,000		50,000	
Kitchen (daily meals served)	2 meals/ day	3,000		3,000	
Fitness/rehab/wellness (daily visits)	45+ users	3,200		3,200	
Pool(s) and related areas (users)	5–30 users	2,600		2,600	

RESIDENTIAL FACILITIES

Project element	apartments		
	no.	typical size GSF	size range GSF
One bedroom units	107	958	800–1,129
Two bedroom units	48	1,236	1,236
Two bedroom plus den units	101	1,533	1,376–1,724
Total (all units)	259		347,000
Guest apartments	3	325	325
Residents' social areas (lounges, dining, and recreation spaces)			50,000
Medical/health/fitness and activities areas			7,000
Administrative, public, and ancillary support service areas			67,000
Service, maintenance, and mechanical areas			19,000
Total gross area			490,000

ASSISTED LIVING FACILITIES
General social/residential assisted living models

Project element	new construction		renovations	
	no. units	typical size GSF	no. units	typical size GSF
Small	24	550		
Medium	23	600		
Large	12	660		
Extra large	1	730		
Total (all units)	60	36,000		
Residents' social areas (lounges, dining, and recreation spaces)				4,200
Medical, healthcare, therapies, and activities spaces				1,200
Administrative, public, and ancillary support services				2,700
Service, maintenance, and mechanical areas				4,100
Total gross area				59,000

Dementia-specific assisted living models

Project element	new construction		renovations	
	no. units	typical size GSF	no. units	typical size GSF
Small	9	280		
Medium	6	300		
Large	4	330		
Suite	6	600		
Total (all units)	25	9,200		
Residents' social areas (lounges, dining, and recreation spaces)				1,890
Medical, healthcare, therapies and activities spaces				189
Administrative, public, and ancillary support services				1,250
Service, maintenance, and mechanical areas				795
Total gross area				16,000

NURSING FACILITIES
Skilled nursing facilities

Project element	new construction		renovations
	no. beds	typical room size GSF	typical room size GSF
Residents in one-bed/ single rooms	60	280	
Residents in one-bed/ double rooms	6	560	
No. of residents 66			
rooms 72			
beds	66	20,000	
Social areas (lounges, dining, and recreation spaces)			3,100
Medical, healthcare, therapies, and activities spaces			850
Administrative, public, and ancillary support services			1,800
Service, maintenance, and mechanical areas			1,350
Total gross area			35,300

CONSTRUCTION COSTS

The following information is based on actual costs

Building costs
Total building costs $66 M
Total project cost   Not available

EPISCOPAL CHURCH HOME

Status of project: Completed March 2003
Facility administrator: Keith R. Knapp
Owner: Trustees of the Church Home and Infirmary, Inc. d/b/a Episcopal Church Home
Architect: Reese Design Collaborative, PSC
Interior designer: Reese Design Collaborative, PSC
Structural engineer: American Engineers, Inc.
Mechanical engineer: Kerr–Greulich Engineers, Inc.
Electrical engineer: Kerr–Greulich Engineers, Inc.
Civil engineer: American Engineers, Inc.
Contractor: Lloyd Bilyeu Construction Company, Inc.

PROJECT AREAS

Project element	included in this project				
	units, beds, or clients	new GSF	renovated GSF	total gross area	total on site or served by project
Cottages/villas (units)	36			50,400	42
Senior living/assisted living/ personal care (units)	75			17,200	30
Special care for persons with dementia	52	38,000			52
Skilled nursing care (beds)	139			31,600	139
Common social areas		12,000		20,000	210
Kitchen (daily meals served)	700			2,800	700

ASSISTED LIVING FACILITIES
Dementia-specific assisted living models

Project element	new construction	
	no. units	typical size
Studio units	52	243
Total (all units)	52	13,520
Residents' social areas (lounges, dining, and recreation spaces)		11,290
Medical, healthcare, therapies, and activities spaces		16,940
Administrative, public, and ancillary support services		11,420
Service, maintenance, and mechanical areas		4,830
Total gross area		58,000

CONSTRUCTION COSTS

The following information is based on actual costs
Final construction cost as of August 2003
Financing sources: non-taxable bond offering

> **Building costs**
> Total building costs $6.79 M
> **Site costs**
> Total site costs $333,270
> **Total project costs**   **$8.06 M**

FRIENDSHIP VILLAGE OF SCHAUMBURG

Status of project: Estimated completion date September 2006
Facility administrator: Robert Alston
Owner: Friendship Village of Schaumburg
Architect: DORSKY HODGSON + PARTNERS, Inc.
Associate architects: Jaeger Nickola Associates Ltd.
Interior designer: DORSKY HODGSON + PARTNERS, Inc.
Landscape architect: Hitchcock Design Group
Structural engineer: Shenberger and Associates, Inc.
Mechanical engineer: Karpinski Engineering
Electrical engineer: Karpinski Engineering
Civil engineer: Infracon, Inc.
Contractor: Phase I: A.J. Maggio Construction Co.

PROJECT AREAS

Project element	included in this project				
	units, beds, or clients	new GSF	renovated GSF	total gross area	total on site or served by project
Apartments (units)	170	194,200		194,200	699*
Cottages/villas (units)	28	49,600		49,600	28
Senior living/assisted living/personal care (units)					195
Special care for persons with dementia					44
Skilled nursing care (beds)					206
Common social areas (people)		23,400			23,400
Kitchen (daily meals served)		2,700			2,700
Retail space (shops/ restaurants, etc)		14,900			14,900
Fitness/rehab/wellness (daily visits)		4,900			4,900
Pool(s) and related areas (users)		10,600			10,600

*The independent units will be at this peak number after phase II construction and before phase III renovations begin.

RESIDENTIAL FACILITIES

Project element	cottages			apartments		
	no.	typical size GSF	size range GSF	no.	typical size GSF	size range GSF
One bedroom units				90	800	755–965
Two bedroom units	14	1,350	1,350	80	1,075	1,050–1,110
Two bedroom plus den units	14	1,750	1,750			
Total (all units)	28	49,600		170	149,900	
Residents' social areas (lounges, dining, and recreation spaces)					38,300	
Medical/health/fitness and activities areas					15,500	
Administrative, public, and ancillary support service areas					47,300	
Service, maintenance, and mechanical areas					11,500	
Total gross area					262,400	

OTHER FACILITIES

Project element	new construction		
	no.	size	
Friendship Center	1	13,800	
Underground parking garage	1	39,100	

FRIENDSHIP VILLAGE OF SCHAUMBURG (CONTINUED)

CONSTRUCTION COSTS

The following information is based on contractor's estimates and bids

Building costs

Total building costs, phase I	$6 M
Total building costs, phase II	$40 M
Total building costs, combined	$46 M
Site costs	
Total site costs, phase I	$1.5 M
Total site costs, phase II	$4 M
Total site costs, combined	$5.5 M
Total project costs	
Phase I project costs	$8 M
Phase II project costs	$51 M
Total project costs	**$59 M**

THE GARLANDS OF BARRINGTON

Status of project: Completed phase I 2002
Facility administrator: Tom Herb
Owner: Barrington Venture, LLC
Architect: Torti Gallas and Partners • CHK, Inc
Interior designer: Kenneth E. Hurd & Associates
Landscape architect: Joe Karr & Associates and Harry Weese Associates
Structural engineer: Smislova Kehnemui & Associates
Mechanical engineer: Environmental Systems Design, Inc.
Electrical engineer: Environmental Systems Design, Inc.
Civil engineer: Gewalt Hamilton Associates
Contractor: Pepper Construction Company

PROJECT AREAS

Project element	included in this project				
	units, beds, or clients	new GSF	renovated GSF	total gross area	total on site or served by project
Apartments (units)	271			385,032	
Cottages/villas (units)	26 villas			50,400	
Senior living/assisted living/personal care (units)	69 units			36,789	
Special care for persons with dementia	20 units			16,374	
Skilled nursing care (beds)	19 beds			15,990	
Common social areas	6 public living rooms, library, clinic, lounge, pool room, arts and crafts, swimming pool, 2 hair salons, spa with massage, sauna and gymnasium				
Kitchen (daily meals served)	3 meals				
Retail space (shops/restaurants, etc)	3 restaurants, bank, gift shop, 2 outdoor cafes, consignment store				
Fitness/rehab/wellness (daily visits)	1 fitness center open all day				
Building H/spa under construction	1 health care center containing a clinic, dementia units, skilled nursing and assisted living units				
Pool(s) and related areas (users)	8,639	2,243		10,882	
Other part of phase 1 ILU	12 guest rooms			3,680	

RESIDENTIAL FACILITIES
Independent living units

Project element	cottages			apartments	
	no.	typical size GSF	size range GSF	typical size GSF	size range GSF
One bedroom units				15	890–1,000
Two bedroom units				20	1,140–1,520
Two bedroom plus den units				83	1,130–1,814
Three bedroom and den units	26	50,400		53	2,050–3,000
Total (all units)				171	267,043
Total gross area					385,032

ASSISTED LIVING FACILITIES
General social/residential assisted living models

Project element	new construction		renovations	
	no. units	typical size	no. units	typical size
One bedroom units	27	654		
Two bedroom units	3	935		
Total (all units)	30	21,069		
Residents' social areas (lounges, dining, and recreation spaces)				2,573
Medical, healthcare, therapies, and activities spaces				2,525
Administrative, public, and ancillary support services				5,214
Service, maintenance, and mechanical areas				5,214
Total gross area				36,789

THE GREEN HOUSES AT TRACEWAY™

Status of project: Completed April 2003
Facility administrator: Steve McAlilly
Owner: Mississippi Methodist Senior Services
Architect: The McCarty Company–Design Group, P.A.
Interior designer: The McCarty Company–Design Group, P.A.
Landscape architect: Philips Garden Center
Mechanical engineer: The McCarty Company–Design Group, P.A.
Electrical engineer: The McCarty Company–Design Group, P.A.
Civil engineer: Site Engineering Consultants
Contractor: The McCarty Company–Construction Group, Inc.

Dementia-specific assisted living models

Project element	new construction		renovations
	no. units	typical size	typical size
Typical dementia units	20	407	
Total (all units)	20	8,446	
Residents' social areas (lounges, dining, and recreation spaces)			1,552
Medical, healthcare, therapies and activities spaces			1,066
Administrative, public, and ancillary support services			1,159
Service, maintenance, and mechanical areas			3,122
Total gross area			16,374

NURSING FACILITIES
Skilled nursing facilities

Project element	new construction		renovations
	no. beds	typical room size	typical room size
Residents in one-bed/ single rooms	18	304	
Residents in two-bed/ double rooms	1	433	
Total	19	5,974	
Social areas (lounges, dining, recreation, and activities spaces)			2,607
Medical, healthcare, therapies, administrative, public, and ancillary support services			6,813
Service, maintenance, and mechanical areas			404
Total gross area			15,990

OTHER FACILITIES
Spa and wellness center

Project element	new construction		renovations	
	no.	size	no.	size
Social areas (pool, restaurant, lounges, dining, and recreation spaces)				57,206
Administrative, public, and ancillary support services				Above
Service, maintenance, and mechanical areas				10,613
Total gross area				72,112

CONSTRUCTION COSTS
The following information is based on actual costs, estimates and bids

Building costs
Total building costs $145.2 M
Site costs
Total site costs $15.4 M
Total project costs $157.2 M

PROJECT AREAS

Project element	included in this project				
	units, beds, or clients	new GSF	renovated GSF	total gross area	total on site or served by project
Apartments (units)					102 rooms
Cottages/villas (units)					56 units
Senior living/assisted living/personal care (units)					151 rooms
Skilled nursing care (beds) with dementia *	40	24,160		24,160	140 beds
Common social areas (people)*	40	9,232		9,232	
Kitchen (daily meals served)*	120	864		864	
Fitness/rehab/wellness (daily visits)*	30	360		360	
Service*		3,452		3,452	

* Areas from combined totals of 4 Green Houses in Phase 1 development.

NURSING FACILITIES
Skilled nursing facilities—phase 1 (4 buildings)

Project element	new construction		
	no. beds	typical room size	
Residents in one-bed/ single rooms	40	260	
No. of residents 40 rooms			
40 beds	40	10,424	
Social areas (lounges, dining, and recreation space		10,104	
Medical, healthcare, therapies, and activities spaces		772	
Administrative, public, and ancillary support services		2,496	
Service, maintenance, and mechanical areas		364	
Total gross area		24,160	

CONSTRUCTION COSTS
The following information is based on actual costs
Final construction cost as of August 2003

Building costs (phase 1 only)
Total building costs $2.3 M
Site costs
Total site costs $558,341
Total project costs $3.2 M

Handmaker Jewish Services for the Aging – Rubin Campus

Status of project: Completed November 2002
Facility administrator: Lee Olitzky
Owner: Handmaker Jewish Services for the Aging
Architect: Gresham & Beach, Architects
Associate architect: Lizard Rock Designs, LLC
Interior designer: Interior Technologies
Landscape architect: Guy Greene
Structural engineer: Holben, Martin & White
Mechanical engineer: SMU Mechanical Engineering
Electrical engineer: Stantec
Civil engineer: Stantec
Contractor: T.L. Roof

Project element	included in this project			
	units, beds, or clients	new GSF	renovated GSF	total gross area	total on site or served by project
Cottages/villas	14		9,475	9,475	9,475
Senior living/assisted living/personal care (units)	90	56,772		56,772	56,772
Special care for persons with dementia	32	17,520		17,520	17,520
Skilled nursing care (beds)	48	16,918		16,918	16,918
Common social areas (people)		31,650		31,650	31,650
Kitchen (daily meals served)	250	4,266		4,266	4,266
Elder day care (clients)	100	10,218		10,218	10,218
Retail space (shops/restaurants, etc)		250		250	250
Other Laundry, materials management, staff lockers		4,350		4,350	4,350

RESIDENTIAL FACILITIES

Project element	cottages				apartments		
	no.	typical size GSF	size range GSF		no.	typical size GSF	size range GSF
One bedroom units					14	675	550–700
Total (all units)					14	9,475	
Total gross area						9,475	

ASSISTED LIVING FACILITIES

Project element	new construction			renovations		
	no.	typical size GSF	size range GSF	no.	typical size GSF	size range GSF
Studio units	8	350				
One bedroom units	38	525				
Two bedroom units	8	725				
Total (all units)	54	28,550				
Residents' social areas (lounges, dining, and recreation spaces)				4,000		
Medical, healthcare, therapies, and activities spaces				2,800		
Administrative, public, and ancillary support services				500		
Service, maintenance, and mechanical areas				700		
Total gross area				45,752		

Dementia-specific assisted living models

Project element	new construction			renovations		
	no.	typical size GSF	size range GSF	no.	typical size GSF	size range GSF
One bedroom units	16	475				
Total (all units)	16	3,800				
Residents' social areas (lounges, dining, and recreation spaces)				2,000		
Medical, healthcare, therapies, and activities spaces				800		
Total gross area				8,760		

Medical assisted living models

Project element	new construction			renovations		
	no.	typical size GSF	size range GSF	no.	typical size GSF	size range GSF
Shared/double units	16	475				
Single occupancy units	4	350				
Total (all units)	26	9,000				
Residents' social areas (lounges, dining, and recreation spaces)				2,650		
Medical, healthcare, therapies, and activities spaces				350		
Administrative, public, and ancillary support services				2,180		
Service, maintenance, and mechanical areas				7,000		
Total gross area				24,000		

NURSING FACILITIES

Dementia care–skilled nursing facilities

Project element	new construction		renovations	
	no. beds	typical room size	no. beds	typical room size
Residents in two-bed/double rooms	16	475		
No. of residents 16 rooms 8				
beds	16	3,800		
Social areas (lounges, dining, and recreation spaces)				2,000
Medical, healthcare, therapies, and activities spaces				800
Total gross area				8,760

Sub-acute care facilities

Project element	new construction		renovations	
	no. beds	typical room size	no. beds	typical room size
Residents in one-bed/single rooms	10	325		
Residents in two-bed/double rooms	32	375		
No. of residents 42 rooms 26				
beds	42	7,900		
Social areas (lounges, dining, and recreation spaces)				1,000
Administrative, public, and ancillary support services				500
Total gross area				14,100

Hospice care facilities

Project element	new construction		renovations	
	no. beds	typical room size GSF	no. beds	typical room size GSF
Residents in one-bed/single rooms	6	325		
No. of residents 6 Rooms 6				
Beds	6	1,950		
Social areas (lounges, dining, and recreation spaces)				225
Administrative, public, and ancillary support services				150
Total gross area				2,900

OTHER FACILITIES

Project element	new construction		renovations	
	no.	size GSF	no.	size GSF
Adult day care center	1	6,496		
Adult day care center–dementia			1	3,792

CONSTRUCTION COSTS

Building costs
Total building costs $10.9 M

Site costs
Total site costs $800,000

Total project costs $13 M

HEBREW HOME OF GREATER WASHINGTON: SMITH–KOGOD BUILDING

Status of project: Completed May 2003
Facility administrator: Warren Slavin
Owner: Hebrew Home of Greater Washington
Architect: Perkins Eastman
Interior designer: Perkins Eastman
Landscape architect: O'Dougherty Graham Landscape Arch
Structural engineer: AMN Engineers
Mechanical engineer: Cosentini Associates
Electrical engineer: Cosentini Associates
Contractor: Triad Construction

PROJECT AREAS

Project element	included in this project				
	units, beds, or clients	new GSF	renovated GSF	total gross area	total on site or served by project
Skilled nursing care (beds)	282	55,000			55,000
Common social areas (people)		5,500	40,000		45,500
Kitchen (daily meals served)	3 meals/ day		1,039 pantry		1,039 pantry
Service/offices			31,500		31,500

NURSING FACILITIES
Skilled nursing facilities

Project element	renovations		
	no. beds	typical room size	GSF
Residents in one-bed/ single rooms	156	195	32,000
Residents in two-bed/ double rooms	126	345	23,000
Social areas (lounges, dining, and recreation spaces)		5,500	solarium/dining
Medical, healthcare, therapies, and activities spaces			50,000
Administrative, public, and ancillary support services			3,000
Service, maintenance, and mechanical areas			31,500
Total gross area		5,350	155,000

CONSTRUCTION COSTS

The following information is based on actual costs
Financing sources: private donations and fundraising

Building costs
Total building costs .... $9.25 M
Site costs
Total site costs $156,910
Total project costs .... **$10.1 M**

HOLY FAMILY VILLAGE

Status of project: Completed September 2001
Facility administrator: Roberta Magurany
Owner: Catholic Charities
Architect: Nagle Hartray Danker Kagan McKay Penney Architects Ltd.
Interior designer: Eva Maddox & Associates/Jeanne Hartnett & Associates
Landscape architect: Wolff Clements & Associates
Structural engineer: Beer Gorski & Graff, Inc.
Mechanical engineer: WMA Consulting Engineers, Ltd.
Electrical engineer: WMA Consulting Engineers, Ltd.
Civil engineer: Eriksson Engineering Associates, Ltd.
Contractor: Skender Construction Company/Paul Borg Construction

PROJECT AREAS

Project element	included in this project				
	units, beds, or clients	new GSF	renovated GSF	total gross area	total on site or served by project
Senior living/assisted living/personal care (units)	18	9,180		9,180	18
Skilled nursing care (beds)	99	15,570		15,570	99
Common social areas (people)	99	4,714		4714	99
Kitchen (daily meals served)	350	1,765		1,765	350
Fitness/rehab/wellness (daily visits)	99	1,345		1,345	99
Chapel	200	2,134		2,134	200

ASSISTED LIVING FACILITIES
General social/residential assisted living models

Project element	new construction		renovations
	no. units	typical size GSF	typical size GSF
One bedroom units	18	510	
Total (all units)	18	9,180	
Residents' social areas (lounges, dining, and recreation spaces)			2,630
Medical, healthcare, therapies, and activities spaces			420
Administrative, public, and ancillary support services			100
Service, maintenance, and mechanical areas			4,800
Total gross area			26,368

NURSING FACILITIES
Skilled nursing facilities

Project element	new construction		renovations
	no. beds	typical room size GSF	typical room size GSF
Residents in one-bed/ single rooms	3	190	
Residents in two-bed/ double rooms	48	330	
Residents share multi-bed rooms/wards	48	295	
No. of residents 99 rooms 51 beds	99		
Social areas (lounges, dining, and recreation spaces)			4,716
Medical, healthcare, therapies, and activities spaces			1,345
Administrative, public, and ancillary support services			2,000
Service, maintenance, and mechanical areas			1,500
Total gross area			51,825

HOLY FAMILY VILLAGE (CONTINUED)

CONSTRUCTION COSTS

The following information is based on actual costs

Building costs

Total building costs	$12.6 M

Site costs

Total site costs	$1.5 M
Total project costs	**$15.9 M**

HUNTERBROOK RIDGE AND THE SEABURY AT FIELDHOME

Status of project: Completed September 2002
Facility administrator: Gary Brueilly
Owner: Field Home Holy Comforter
Architect: Perkins Eastman
Interior designer: Perkins Eastman
Landscape architect: Divney Tung Schwalbe
Structural engineer: Gilsanz Murray Steficek LLP
Mechanical engineer: Robert Ettinger Associates
Electrical engineer: Robert Ettinger Associates
Civil engineer: Divney Tung Schwalbe
Contractor: LeCesse Construction

PROJECT AREAS

Project element	included in this project				
	units, beds, or clients	new GSF	renovated GSF	total gross area	total on site or served by project
Cottages/villas (units)	64	104,160		104,160	104,160
Senior living/assisted living/personal care (units)	40	37,760		37,760	37,760
Continuing-care retirement communities (units)	40	22,210		22,210	22,210

RESIDENTIAL FACILITIES

Project element	cottages		
	no.	typical size GSF	
One bedroom/den units	24	1,510	
Two bedroom units	40	1,700	
Total (all units)	64	104,160	

ASSISTED LIVING FACILITIES
General social/residential assisted living models

Project element	new construction	
	no. units	typical size GSF
Studio units	10	350
One bedroom units	28	540
Two bedroom units	2	920
Total (all units)	40	20,475
Residents' social areas (lounges, dining and recreation spaces)		3,745
Medical, healthcare, therapies, and activities spaces		1,000
Administrative, public and ancillary support services		1,345
Service, maintenance, and mechanical areas		2,900
Total gross area		37,760

Dementia-specific assisted living models

Project element	new construction	
	no. units	typical size GSF
Studio units	40	200
Total (all units)	40	8,000
Residents' social areas (lounges, dining, and recreation spaces)		5,125
Medical, healthcare, therapies, and activities spaces		790
Administrative, public, and ancillary support services		230
Service, maintenance, and mechanical areas		900
Total gross area		22,210

CONSTRUCTION COSTS

The following information is based on estimates

Financing sources: non-taxable bond offering

Building costs

Total building costs	$12.49 M

Site costs

Total site costs	$3.72 M
Total project costs	**$18.62 M**

KEYSTONE COMMUNITY

Status of project: Completed March 2003
Owner: Keystone Communities
Architect: Nelson•Tremain Partnership
Interior designer: Sterling Interior Design
Landscape architect: HTPO, Inc
Structural engineer: Van Sickle, Allen & Associates, Inc.
Mechanical engineer: Allman & Assoc., Inc
Electrical engineer: Allman & Assoc., Inc
Civil engineer: HTPO, Inc
Contractor: Weis Builders

PROJECT AREAS

Project element	included in this project				
	units, beds, or clients	new GSF	renovated GSF	total gross area	total on site or served by project
Senior living/assisted living/personal care (units)	42 units	25,104		25,104	
Special care for persons with dementia	20 units	5,660		5,660	
Common social areas (people)	66	5,250		5,250	
Kitchen (daily meals served)	3 meals/ day	830		830	200 meals daily
Fitness/rehab/wellness (daily visits)		1,300		1,300	
Beauty salon		172		172	

ASSISTED LIVING FACILITIES
General social/residential assisted living models

Project element	new construction		
	no. units	typical size GSF	
Studio units	16	540	
One bedroom units	22	599	
Two bedroom units	4	816	
Total (all units)	42	25,104	
Residents' social areas (lounges, dining, and recreation spaces)		2,900	
Medical, healthcare, therapies, and activities spaces		1,481	
Administrative, public, and ancillary support services		1,633	
Service, maintenance, and mechanical areas		2,886	
Total gross area includes corridors, stairs, elevators		46,200	

Dementia-specific assisted living models

Project element	new construction		
	no. units	typical size GSF	
Studio units (small studio)	14	240	
Large studio	6	383	
Total (all units)	20	5,660	
Residents' social areas (lounges, dining, and recreation spaces)		1,976	
Medical, healthcare, therapies, and activities spaces		110	
Administrative, public, and ancillary support services		352	
Service, maintenance, and mechanical areas		265	
Total gross area		10,412	

CONSTRUCTION COSTS

The following information is based on actual costs
Final construction cost as of March 2003
Financing sources: HUD 232 assisted living loan 90%, private funding 10%

Building costs
Total building costs $4.7 M
Site costs
Total site cost $208,525
Total project costs   **$6.4 M**

LASELL VILLAGE

Status of project: Completed July 2000
Facility administrator: Jim Wingardner
Owner: Lasell College
Architect: Steffian Bradley Architects
Interior designer: Steffian Bradley Architects
Landscape architect: Carol R. Johnson Associates, Inc.
Structural engineer: Charles Chaloff Consulting Engineering
Mechanical engineer: Zade Company, Inc.
Electrical engineer: Zade Company, Inc.
Civil engineer: Rizzo Assocites, Inc.
Contractor: Suffolk Building Corporation

PROJECT AREAS

Project element	included in this project				
	units, beds, or clients	new GSF	renovated GSF	total gross area	total on site or served by project
Continuing-care retirement communities	162 units	270,000		270,000	270,000
Skilled nursing care (beds)	44	11,550		11,500	11,550
Common social areas (people)	± 250	24,000		24,000	24,000
Kitchen (daily meals served) (3 meals: breakfast, lunch, dinner)	2,600			2,236	
Retail space (shops/ restaurants, etc)			1,600	1,600	1,600
Pool(s) and related areas (users)			3,600	3,600	3,600

RESIDENTIAL FACILITIES

Project element	cottages		apartments		
	no.	typical size GSF	size range GSF	no.	typical size GSF	size range GSF
One bedroom units				79	990	690–1,115
Two bedroom units				57	1,115	1,010–1,135
Two bedroom plus den units				26	1,230	1,175–1,260
Total (all units)		200,000	162			
Residents' social areas (lounges, dining, and recreation spaces)					24,800	
Medical/health/fitness and activities areas					11,536	
Administrative, public, and ancillary support service areas					4,700	
Service, maintenance, and mechanical areas					21,866	
Total gross area					270,000	

NURSING FACILITIES
Skilled nursing facilities

Project element	new construction		renovations
	no. beds	typical room size GSF	typical room size GSF
Residents in one-bed/ single rooms	7	240	
Residents in two-bed/ double rooms	19	308	
No. of residents 44			
rooms 26			
beds 44			1,000
Medical, healthcare, therapies, and activities spaces			1,600
Administrative, public, and ancillary support services			2,700
Service, maintenance, and mechanical areas			2,500
Total gross area			14,222

La Vida Real

Status of project: Completed July 2003
Facility administrator: Dixie King
Owner: Senior Resource Group, LLC
Architect: Mithun
Interior designer: Martha Child Interiors
Landscape architect: IVY Landscape Architects, Inc.
Structural engineer: Putnam Collins & Scott Associates
Mechanical engineer: HV engineering
Electrical engineer: Travis Fitzmaurice Associates
Civil engineer: Stuart engineering
Contractor: Swinerton Builders

PROJECT AREAS

Project element	included in this project				
	units, beds, or clients	new GSF	renovated GSF	total gross area	total on site or served by project
Apartments (units)	210	166,328			166,328
Senior living/assisted living/personal care (units)	98	64,458			64,458
Special care for persons with dementia	14	5,403			5,403
Common social areas (people)		19,724			19,724
Kitchen (daily meals served)		36,985			36,985
Fitness/rehab/wellness (daily visits)		913			913
Pool(s) and related areas (users)		6,643			6,643

RESIDENTIAL FACILITIES

Project element	apartments		
	no.	typical size GSF	size range GSF
Studio units	14	469	457–499
One bedroom units	105	669	669
Two bedroom units	69	905	905–1,057
Two bedroom plus den units	22	1,125	1,126–1,142
Total (all units)	210		166,328
Residents' social areas (lounges, dining, and recreation spaces)		11,252	
Medical/health/fitness and activities areas		5,684	
Administrative, public, and ancillary support service areas		4,603	
Service, maintenance, and mechanical areas		14,388	
Total gross area		249,946	

ASSISTED LIVING FACILITIES
General social/residential assisted living models

Project element	new construction		renovations
	no. units	typical size	typical size
Studio units	39	470	
One bedroom units	48	586	
Total (all units)	98	64,458	
Residents' social areas (lounges, dining, and recreation spaces)			6,905
Medical, healthcare, therapies, and activities spaces			1,842
Administrative, public, and ancillary support services			2,456
Service, maintenance, and mechanical areas			1,580
Total gross area			93,466

Dementia-specific assisted living models

Project element	new construction		renovations
	no. units	typical size	typical size
Studio units	3	470	
Two room studio	11	481	
Total (all units)	14	5,403	
Residents' social areas (lounges, dining, and recreation spaces)			1,567
Medical, healthcare, therapies, and activities spaces			65
Administrative, public, and ancillary support services			288
Service, maintenance, and mechanical areas			157
Total gross area			9,808

CONSTRUCTION COSTS
The following information is based on actual costs

Final construction cost as of August 2003

Building costs

Total building costs	$40 M
Total project costs	**$52 M**

Marsh's Edge

Status of project: Estimated completion date March 2006
Facility administrator: Father Douglas Renagar
Owner: Coastal Community Retirement Corporation
Architect: Cochran, Stephenson & Donkervoet, Inc.
Interior designer: Stanzione Associates
Landscape architect: The Sea Island Company
Structural engineer: Morabito Consultants
Mechanical engineer: James Posey Associates
Electrical engineer: James Posey Associates
Civil engineer: Thomas & Hutton Engineering Co.
Contractor: Weitz Construction

PROJECT AREAS

Project element	included in this project				
	units, beds, or clients	new GSF	renovated GSF	total gross area	total on site or served by project
Apartments (units)	114	212,658		212,658	114
Cottages/villas (units)	30	94,130		94,130	30
Senior living/assisted living/personal care (units)	20	19,147		19,147	20
Special care for persons with dementia	12	7,358		7,358	12
Skilled nursing care (beds)	20	16,732		16,732	20
Common social areas (people)	692	30,420		30,420	692
Kitchen (daily meals served)				2,944	
Fitness/rehab/wellness (daily visits)		404		404	
Pool(s) and related areas (users)		4,808		4,808	

RESIDENTIAL FACILITIES

Project element	apartments		
	no.	typical size GSF	size range GSF
Studio units (guest)	2	310	310
One bedroom units	14	1029	822–1,029
Two bedroom units	86	1446	1,386–1,625
Two bedroom plus den units	24	1500	1,260–1,886
Total (all units)		165,184	
Residents' social areas (lounges, dining, and recreation spaces)		10,050	
support Administrative, public, and ancillary service areas (storage)		6,922	
Service, maintenance, and mechanical areas		29,280	
Total gross area		212,658	

ASSISTED LIVING FACILITIES
General social/residential assisted living models

Project element	new construction		
	no.units	typical size	
Studio units	1	598	
One bedroom units	19	535	
Total (all units)	20	10,763	
Residents' social areas (lounges, dining, and recreation spaces)		1,835	
Medical, healthcare, therapies, and activities spaces		759	
Administrative, public, and ancillary support services		810	
Service, maintenance, and mechanical areas		793	
Total gross area		14,960	

Dementia-specific assisted living models

Project element	new construction		
	no. units	typical size	
One bedroom units	12	210	
Total (all units)	12	2,520	
Residents' social areas (lounges, dining, and recreation spaces)		1,600	
Medical, healthcare, therapies, and activities spaces		300	
Administrative, public, and ancillary support services		250	
Service, maintenance, and mechanical areas		200	
Total gross area		4,870	

NURSING FACILITIES
Skilled nursing facilities

Project element	new construction		
	no. beds	typical room size	
Residents in one-bed/ single rooms	20	240	
No. of residents rooms 20			
beds 20		4,800	
Social areas (lounges, dining, and recreation spaces)		3,820	
Medical, healthcare, therapies, and activities spaces		780	
Administrative, public, and ancillary support services		1,678	
Service, maintenance, and mechanical areas		772	
Total gross area		16,732	

CONSTRUCTION COSTS
The following information is based on contractor's estimates

Building costs
Total building costs $46.7 M
Site costs
Total site costs $6M
Total project costs   Not available

MASONIC VILLAGE AT SEWICKLEY

Status of project: Completed October 2003
Facility administrator: B.J. Franks
Owner: Masonic Homes of the Grand Lodge
Architect: Perkins Eastman
Interior designer: Perkins Eastman
Landscape architect: Graham Landscape Architecture
Structural engineer: Atlantic Engineering Services
Mechanical engineer: Dodson Engineering, Inc
Electrical engineer: Carl J. Long & Associates
Civil engineer: The Gateway Engineers
Contractor: NDC Builders, LLC

PROJECT AREAS

Project element	included in this project				
	units, beds, or clients	new GSF	renovated GSF	total gross area	total on site or served by project
Apartments (units)	228	304,250		305,250	305,250
Cottages/villas (units)	35	91,000			91,000
Senior living/assisted living/personal care (units)	60	80,000	5,000	85,000	85,000
Continuing-care retirement communities	1				
Skilled nursing care (beds)	128	1,500	67,600	67,600	67,600
Common social areas (people)	350	5,940		8,125	8,125
Kitchen (daily meals served)	3	1,400			1,400
Children's day care (clients)	40	7,500		7,500	7,500
Retail space (shops/restaurants, etc)	6	4,200		4,200	4,200
Fitness/rehab/wellness (daily visits) includes pool	1	12,000			12,000

RESIDENTIAL FACILITIES

Project element	cottages			apartments	
	no.	typical size GSF	size range GSF	no.	
Two bedroom plus den units	17	1,981	1,981–3,113		
Three bedroom and larger units	18	3,286	2,376–3,286		
Total (all units)	35			228	

ASSISTED LIVING FACILITIES
General social/residential assisted living models

Project element	new construction		renovations	
	no. units	typical size GSF	no. units	typical size GSF
Studio units	44	375		16,500
One bedroom units	16	515		8,250
Total (all units)	60			24,740
Residents' social areas (lounges, dining, and recreation spaces)				9,000
Medical, healthcare, therapies, day care, and activities spaces				25,250
Administrative, public, and ancillary support services				7,200
Service, maintenance, and mechanical areas				11,435
Total gross area				80,105

NURSING FACILITIES
Skilled nursing facilities

Project element		renovations	
		no. beds	typical room size
Residents in one-bed/single rooms		8	270
Residents in two-bed/double rooms		120	270
No. of residents	128		
rooms	64		
beds	128		

OTHER FACILITIES

Project element	new construction	
	no.	size
Community center	1	48,000
Wellness center	1	12,000

CONSTRUCTION COSTS

The following information is based on actual costs

Building costs
Total building costs $59.2 M
Site costs
Total site costs $7.2 M
Total project costs $70 M

MERCY RIDGE

Status of project: Completed July 2001 Phase I
Facility administrator: Sr. Helen Amos
Owner: Mercy Ridge, Inc
Architect: Cochran, Stephenson & Donkervoet, Inc.
Interior designer: Rita St. Clair Associates, Inc.
Landscape architect: Daft-McCune-Walker
Structural engineer: Morabito Consultants
Mechanical engineer: James Posey Associates, Inc.
Electrical engineer: James Posey Associates, Inc.
Civil engineer: Daft-McCune-Walker, Inc.
Contractor: Harkins Builders, Inc.

PROJECT AREAS

Project element	included in this project				
	units, beds, or clients	new GSF	renovated GSF	total gross area	total on site or served by project
Apartments (units)	259	420,000		420,000	259
Senior living/assisted living/personal care (units)	18	21,000		21,000	18
Special care for persons with dementia	12	6,500		6,500	12
Common social areas (people)	375	20,000		20,000	375
Kitchen (daily meals served)	450	4,000		4,000	450
Retail space (shops/ restaurants, etc)	3	3,000		3,000	3
Fitness/rehab/wellness (daily visits)	30	1,500		1,500	30

RESIDENTIAL FACILITIES

Project element	apartments	
	no.	typical size GSF*
Studio units	10	665
One bedroom units	70	786
One bedroom plus den units	44	1,000
Two bedroom units	68	1,110
Two bedroom plus den units	41	1,300
Three bedroom and larger units	26	1,600
Total (all units)	259	279,000
Residents' social areas (lounges, dining and recreation spaces)		5,000
Medical/health/fitness and activities areas**		0
Administrative, public, and ancillary support service areas**		0
Service, maintenance, and mechanical areas		8,000
Enclosed parking area		25,000
Total gross area		420,000

*All sizes shown are net areas except total gross area.
**Additional public amenities are included in the Community Center building.

ASSISTED LIVING FACILITIES
General social/residential assisted living models

Project element	new construction		
	no. units	typical size*	
Studio units	10	365	
One bedroom units	8	525	
Total (all units)	18	7,850	
Residents' social areas (lounges, dining, and recreation spaces)		3,200	
Medical, healthcare, therapies, and activities spaces		440	
Administrative, public, and ancillary support services		475	
Service, maintenance, and mechanical areas		1,875	
Total gross area		21,000	
Total net usable area (per space program)		13,850	

*All sizes shown are net areas except total gross area.

Dementia-specific assisted living models

Project element	new construction		
	no. units	typical size*	
Studio units	12	270	
Total (all units)	12	3,240	
Residents' social areas (lounges, dining, and recreation spaces)		975	
Medical, healthcare, therapies, and activities spaces		355	
Total gross area		6,500	
Total net usable area (per space program)		4,570	

*All sizes shown are net areas except total gross area.

OTHER FACILITIES

Project element	new construction	
	no.	size*
Social areas (lounges, dining, and recreation spaces)		16,000
Administrative, public, and ancillary support services		3,800
Service, maintenance, and mechanical areas		14,400
Total gross area		50,000
Total net usable area (per space program)		34,200
Overall gross/net factor (ratio of gross area/net useable area)		1.46

*All sizes shown are net areas except total gross area.

CONSTRUCTION COSTS

The following information is based on actual costs
Final construction cost as of August 1999
Financing sources: non-taxable bond offering

Building costs	
Total building costs	$40.5 M
Site costs	
Total site costs	$5.5 M
Total project costs	**Not known**

MIRAMONT POINTE

Status of project: Completed February 2002
Facility administrator: Gerald E. Koll
Owner: John B. Goodman LTD. Partnership
Architect: LRS Architects, Inc.
Associate architect: John B. Goodman LTD. Partnership
Interior designer: John B. Goodman LTD. Partnership
Landscape architect: Alpha Engineering, Inc.
Structural engineer: Berry-Nordling Engineers, Inc.
Mechanical engineer: Hunter-Davisson, Inc.
Electrical engineer: New Tech Electric, Inc.
Civil engineer: Alpha Engineering, Inc.
Contractor: Gray-Purcell Contractors

PROJECT AREAS

Project element	included in this project				
	units, beds, or clients	new GSF	renovated GSF	total gross area	total on site or served by project
Senior living/assisted living/personal care (units)	140	98,050		98,050	140
Special care for persons with dementia	14	6,950		6,950	14
Common social areas (people)		64,937		64,937	
Kitchen (daily meals served)		1,456		1,456	
Retail space (shops/ restaurants, etc)		192		192	
Fitness/rehab/ wellness (daily visits)		1,456		1,456	
Pool(s) and related areas (users)		1,664		1,664	
Other					
Bank		120		120	
Wall street room		180		180	
Fireside lounge		540		540	
Piano lounge		640		640	
Concierge		640		640	
Deli/ice cream		320		320	
Country kitchen		1,584		1,584	

ASSISTED LIVING FACILITIES
General social/residential assisted living models

Project element	new construction		
	no. units		typical size GSF
Studio units	470–580	48	525 av
One bedroom units	650–800	86	725 av
Two bedroom units	1,100–2,300	6	1,700
Total (all units)		140	98,050
Residents' social areas (lounges, dining, and recreation spaces)			33,015
Medical, healthcare, therapies, and activities spaces			3,600
Administrative, public, and ancillary support services			4,050
Service, maintenance, and mechanical areas			24,480
Total gross area			163,195

Dementia-specific assisted living models

Project element	new construction		
		no. units	typical size GSF
Studio units	390–540	12	465 av
One bedroom units	640–730	2	685 av
Total (all units)		14	6,950
Residents' social areas (lounges, dining, and recreation spaces)			5,402
Medical, healthcare, therapies and activities spaces			726
Administrative, public and ancillary support services			656
Service, maintenance, and mechanical areas			1,800
Total gross area			15,534

CONSTRUCTION COSTS

Financing sources: taxable bond offering

Site costs
Total site costs $22.7 M
Total project costs   **Owner withheld**

NEWCASTLE PLACE

Status of project: Completed January 2003
Facility administrator: Matt Furno
Owner: Eastcastle Place Inc.
Architect: AG Architecture
Interior designer: Bridget Bohacz & Associates
Landscape architect: Buettner & Associates
Structural engineer: AG Architecture
Mechanical engineer: AG Architecture
Electrical engineer: AG Architecture
Plumbing engineer: AG Architecture
Civil engineer: National Survey and Engineering
Contractor: CG Schmidt

PROJECT AREAS

Project element	included in this project				
	units, beds, or clients	new GSF	renovated GSF	total gross area	total on site or served by project
Apartments (units)	81	85,935			
Cottages/villas (units)	10	15,888			
Senior living/assisted living/personal care (units)	36	22,166			
Special care for persons with dementia	16	3,803			
Skilled nursing care (beds)	47	12,315			
Common social areas (people)	156				
Kitchen (daily meals served)	447				
Pool(s) and related areas (users)	156				

RESIDENTIAL FACILITIES

Project element	cottages			apartments		
	no.	typical size GSF	size range GSF	no.	typical size GSF	size range GSF
One bedroom units				18	771	633–849
Two bedroom units	10	1,718	1,395–1,718	48	1,038	985–1,296
Two bedroom plus den units				9	1,400	1,400
Three bedroom and larger units				6	1,368	1,368
Total (all units)		15,888		81	85,935	
Residents' social areas (lounges, dining, and recreation spaces)					8,622	
Medical/health/fitness and activities areas						
Administrative, public, and ancillary support service areas					5,784	
Service, maintenance, and mechanical areas					4,300	
Total gross area					153,075	

ASSISTED LIVING FACILITIES
General social/residential assisted living models

Project element	new construction	
	no. units	typical size GSF
One bedroom units	34	569
Two bedroom units	2	948
Total (all units)	36	22,166
Residents' social areas (lounges, dining, and recreation spaces)		3,688
Medical, healthcare, therapies, and activities spaces		437
Administrative, public, and ancillary support services		2,827
Service, maintenance, and mechanical areas		1,739
Total gross area		44,533

Dementia-specific assisted living models

Project element	new construction	
	no. units	typical size
Studio units	16	226
Total (all units)	16	3,803
Residents' social areas (lounges, dining, and recreation spaces)		2,057
Medical, healthcare, therapies and activities spaces		74
Administrative, public, and ancillary support services		800
Service, maintenance, and mechanical areas		226
Total gross area		10,515

Skilled nursing facilities

Project element		new construction	
		no. beds	typical room size GSF
Residents in one-bed/single rooms		47	243
No. of residents	47		
rooms	47		
beds		47	12,315
Social areas (lounges, dining, and recreation spaces)	4,594		
Medical, healthcare, therapies, and activities spaces	1,580		
Administrative, public, and ancillary support services	3,700		
Service, maintenance, and mechanical areas			1,721
Total gross area			35,699

OTHER FACILITIES

Project element	new construction
	size
Fitness center	
Social areas (lounges, dining, and recreation spaces)	4,589
Administrative, public, and ancillary support services	1,777
Service, maintenance, and mechanical areas	260
Total gross area	6,711

CONSTRUCTION COSTS

The following information is based on actual costs
Final construction cost as of March 2003
Financing sources: non-taxable bond offering and owner equity

Building costs
Total building costs $32.12 M
Total project costs $37.76 M

NICARRY MEETINGHOUSE

Status of project: Completed September 2001
Facility administrator: Vernon L. King, president
Owner: The Brethren Home Community
Architect: Reese, Lower, Patrick & Scott, Ltd.
Interior designer: Reese, Lower, Patrick & Scott, Ltd.
Landscape architect: Reese, Lower, Patrick & Scott, Ltd./
Derck & Edson Associates
Structural engineer: Parfitt/Ling
Mechanical engineer: Erdman Anthony Associates, Inc.
Electrical engineer: Reese Engineering, Inc.
Civil engineer: Land Survey Consultants, Inc.
Contractor: Warfel Construction Company

CONSTRUCTION COSTS
Total project costs $1.8 M

OUR LADY OF VICTORY CONVENT

Status of project: Completed November 2002
Owner: The Franciscan Sisters of Chicago
Architect: The Troyer Group, Inc.
Interior designer: The Troyer Group, Inc.
Landscape architect: The Troyer Group, Inc.
Structural engineer: Abatangelo-Hason, Ltd.
Mechanical engineer: The Troyer Group, Inc.
Electrical engineer: The Troyer Group, Inc.
Civil engineer: The Troyer Group, Inc.
Contractor: Henry Brothers, Co.

PROJECT AREAS

Project element	included in this project				
	units, beds, or clients	new GSF	renovated GSF	total gross area	total on site or served by project
Senior living/assisted living/personal care (units)	72	29,500		29,500	82
Common social areas (people)		17,800		17,800	
Kitchen (daily meals served)		2,400		2,400	
Retail space (shops/restaurants, etc)		700		700	
Fitness/rehab/wellness (daily visits)		1,600		1,600	

CONSTRUCTION COSTS
The following information is based on actual costs
Final construction cost as of December 2002
Total project costs   Not available

PACE at St. Cecilia

Status of project: Estimated completion date June 2005
Facility administrator: Anne Witmer (acting)
Owner: Social Apostolate of the Archdiocese of New Orleans
Architect: Blitch/Knevel Architects, Inc.
Interior designer: Blitch/Knevel Architects, Inc.
Landscape architect: Blitch/Knevel Architects, Inc.
Structural engineer: Jeffrey Thomas Avegno
Mechanical engineer: MCC Services
Electrical engineer: Northshore Electric
Civil engineer: Jeffrey Thomas Avegno
Contractor: Milton Womack Construction Co.

PROJECT AREAS

Project element	included in this project				
	units, beds, or clients	new GSF	renovated GSF	total gross area	total on site or served by project
Other (please decscribe) PACE program Program of All-inclusive Care for the Elderly	120 clients	2,975	14,750	17,725	120 clients

OTHER FACILITIES–PACE PROGRAM

Project element	new construction		renovations	
	no.	size GSF	no.	size GSF
Main activity space				6,200
Special care (dementia) activity space				1,600
Satchmo café				700
Basin St. health club		1,200		
Therapy garden		1,600		
Clinic				3,035
Social areas (lounges, dining, and recreation spaces)		(Above)		
Administrative, public, and ancillary support services				2,200
Service, maintenance and mechanical areas				1,200
Total gross area				17,725

CONSTRUCTION COSTS

The following information is based on actual costs

Building costs
Total building costs $2.2 M

Piper Shores

Status of project: Completed October 2001
Facility administrator: Deb Riddell
Owner: Maine Life Care Retirement Community
Architect: EGA, P.C.
Interior designer: Wellesley Design Consultants
Landscape architect: Richardson Associates
Structural engineer: Shelley Engineering
Mechanical engineer: Yeaton Associates
Electrical engineer: Bartlett Design
Civil engineer: Deluca Hoffman Associates
Contractor: Granger Northern, Inc.

PROJECT AREAS

Project element	included in this project				
	units, beds, or clients	new GSF	renovated GSF	total gross area	total on site or served by project
Apartments (units)	212	270,145		270,145	
Cottages/villas (units)	40	90,120		90,120	

RESIDENTIAL FACILITIES

Project element	cottages			apartments		
	no.	typical size GSF	size range GSF	no.	typical size GSF	size range GSF
Studio units				6	505	240–511
One bedroom units				119	616	527–985
Two bedroom units				75	1,060	718–1243
Two bedroom plus den units	40	2,200	2,000–2,400	52	1,450	1,430–1,460
Total (all units)	40			212		
Total gross area (not including cottages)				270,878		

CONSTRUCTION COSTS

The following information is based on actual costs
Final construction cost as of February 2001

Total project costs   **$26.6 M**

THE STATE VETERANS HOME AT FITZSIMONS

Status of project: Completed July 2002
Owner: State of Colorado, Department of Human Services
Architect: Boulder Associates, Inc.
Associate architect: Luis O. Acosta Architects, P.C.
Interior designer: Boulder Associates, Inc.
Landscape architect: Valerian, LLC
Structural engineer: J.C. Baur & Associates
Mechanical engineer: McGrath, Inc.
Electrical engineer: BCER Engineering, Inc.
Civil engineer: Rocky Mountain Consultants, Inc.
Contractor: Roche Constructors, Inc.

PROJECT AREAS

Project element	included in this project				
	units, beds, or clients	new GSF	renovated GSF	total gross area	total on site or served by project
Skilled nursing care (beds)	180	101,550		101,550	180
Common social areas (people)	180	14,350		14,350	180
Kitchen (daily meals served)	660	3,850		3,850	660
Elder day care (clients)	24	2,150		2,150	24
Fitness/rehab/wellness (daily visits)	40	3,100		3,100	40

NURSING FACILITIES
Skilled nursing facilities

Project element	new construction		renovations
	no. beds	typical room size	typical room size
Residents in one-bed/ single rooms	20	265	
Residents in two-bed/ double rooms	160	425	
No. of residents 180			
rooms 100			
beds	180	39,300	
Social areas (lounges, dining, and recreation spaces)			13,400
Medical, healthcare, therapies, and activities spaces			7,200
Administrative, public, and ancillary support services			19,500
Service, maintenance, and mechanical areas			13,900
Total gross area			125,000

CONSTRUCTION COSTS

The following information is based on actual costs
Financing sources: The Federal VA provided 65 percent of construction costs, FF&E, and some soft costs. The State funded the remaining 35 percent plus all other costs not funded by the VA.

Building costs
Total building costs $20.46 M
Site costs
Total site costs $1.84 M
Total project costs   **$24.84 M**

SUMMIT NURSING HOME

Status of project: Completed June 2004
Facility administrator: Charles E. Rehnborg, LNHA
Owner: Centra Health Systems, Inc
Architect: Hughes Associates Architects
Interior designer: DSM Design Concepts, LLC
Landscape architect: Hughes Associates Architects
Structural engineer: Day & Kinder Consulting Engineers
Mechanical engineer: H.C. Yu and Associates
Electrical engineer: H.C. Yu and Associates
Civil engineer: Hurt & Profitt, Inc.
Contractor: J.E. Jamerson & Sons, Inc.

PROJECT AREAS

Project element	included in this project				
	units, beds, or clients	new GSF	renovated GSF	total gross area	total on site or served by project
Kitchen (daily meals served)		1,822		1,822	

NURSING FACILITIES
Skilled nursing facilities

Project element	new construction		renovations
	no. beds	typical room size GSF	typical room size GSF
Residents in one-bed/ single rooms	24	195	
Residents in two-bed/ double rooms	96	285	
No. of residents 120			
rooms 72			
beds	120	47,355	
Social areas (lounges, dining, and recreation spaces)			4,200
Medical, healthcare, therapies, and activities spaces			1,300
Administrative, public, and ancillary support services			1,800
Service, maintenance, and mechanical areas			5,300
Total gross area			59,955

CONSTRUCTION COSTS

The following information is based on bids

Building costs
Total building costs $6 M
Site costs
Total site costs $581,442
Total project costs   **$6 M**

Sun City Takatsuki

Status of project: Completed September 2001
Facility administrator: Kazushi Inamura
Owner: Half Century More Co.,
Architect: Perkins Eastman
Associate architect: Kanko Kikaku Sekkeisha
Interior designer: Perkins Eastman
Landscape architect: SWA group
Structural engineer: Shell Home
Mechanical engineer: Kenchiku Setsubi Seekei Kenkyusho
Electrical engineer: Kenchiku Setsubi Seekei Kenkyusho
Civil engineer: Kenchiku Setsubi Seekei Kenkyusho
Contractor: Fujiki Komuten

PROJECT AREAS

Project element	included in this project				
	units, beds, or clients	new GSF	renovated GSF	total gross area	total on site or served by project
Apartments (units)	91	640–1,100		60,300	60,300
Senior living/assisted living/personal care (units)	24	445		14,025	14,025
Special care for persons with dementia	34	300		14,025	14,025
Skilled nursing care (beds)	34	300		14,025	14,025
Common social areas (people)	156	11,160		63,100	63,100
Kitchen (daily meals served)	3	3,550		3,550	3,550
Fitness/rehab/wellness (daily visits)		976		976	976

RESIDENTIAL FACILITIES

Project element	apartments		
	no.	typical size GSF	size range GSF
One bedroom units	55	640	640–800
Two bedroom units	37	1,100	740–1,150
Total (all units)	92	63,300	

ASSISTED LIVING FACILITIES
General social/residential assisted living models

Project element	new construction	
	no. units	typical size GSF
One bedroom units	14	340
Two bedroom units	10	640
Total (all units)	24	14,025

Dementia-specific assisted living models

Project element	new construction	
	no. units	typical size GSF
One bedroom units	14	430
Two bedroom units	10	640
Total (all units)	24	14,025

NURSING FACILITIES
Skilled nursing facilities

Project element	new construction	
	no. units	typical size GSF
Residents in one-bed/single rooms	14	340
Residents in two-bed/double rooms	20	765
No. of residents rooms beds	34	14,025

CONSTRUCTION COSTS

The following information is based on actual costs
Final construction cost as of September 2001
Financing sources: private corporation investors/bank

Building costs
Total building costs $32 M
Total project costs   **$32 M**

Sunrise of La Jolla

Status of project: Completed May 2003
Facility administrator: Michelle Pagni
Owner: Sunrise Senior Living
Architect: Mithun
Interior designer: Martha Child Interiors
Landscape architect: IVY Landscape Architects, Inc.
Structural engineer: Putnam Collins & Scott Associates
Mechanical engineer: Westgate Engineering
Electrical engineer: AWA Electrical consultants
Civil engineer: Dudek Associates
Contractor: Suffolk Construction Company, Inc.

PROJECT AREAS

Project element	included in this project				
	units, beds, or clients	new GSF	renovated GSF	total gross area	total on site or served by project
Senior living/assisted living/personal care (units)	31	18,134			18,134
Special care for persons with dementia	19	10,619			10,619
Common social areas (people)		11,041			11,041

ASSISTED LIVING FACILITIES
General social/residential assisted living models

Project element	new construction		renovations
	no. units	typical size	typical size GSF
Studio units	19	300–350	
One bedroom units	8	425–550	
Two bedroom units	4	515–650	
Total (all units)	31	18,134	
Medical, healthcare, therapies, and activities spaces			8,017
Total gross area			26,151

Dementia-specific assisted living models

Project element	new construction		renovations	
	no. units	typical size	no. units	typical size
Studio units	9	300-350		
One bedroom units	7	425-550		
Two bedroom units	3	515-650		
Total (all units)	19	10,619		
Administrative, public, and ancillary support services				3,024
Total gross area				13,643

CONSTRUCTION COSTS

The following information is based on actual costs
Final construction cost as of June 2003

Building costs
Total building costs $8 M
Total project costs   Not known

SUNSET VILLAGE CAFÉ

Status of project: Completed 2002
Facility administrator: Rich Freerksen
Owner: Sunset Association
Architect: Dorsky Hodgson + Partners, Inc.
Interior designer: Dorsky Hodgson + Partners, Inc.
Structural engineer: Hach and Ebersole
Mechanical engineer: Quality Air-Design Build
Electrical engineer: Buist-Design Build
Plumbing engineer: Godwin-Design Build
Civil engineer: Nederveld Associates
Contractor: Fryling Construction

CONSTRUCTION COSTS

The following information is based on actual costs

Total project costs $5.9 M for Café
and Congregate

THE SYLVESTERY AT VINSON HALL

Status of project: Completed January 2003
Facility administrator: Robert DeMaria
Owner: Vinson Hall Corporation
Architect: Reese, Lower, Patrick & Scott, Ltd.
Interior designer: Reese, Lower, Patrick & Scott, Ltd.
Landscape architect: Reese, Lower, Patrick & Scott, Ltd.
Structural engineer: Parfitt/Ling
Mechanical engineer: Consolidated Engineers
Electrical engineer: Consolidated Engineers
Civil engineer: Vika, Inc.
Contractor: HITT Contracting, Inc

PROJECT AREAS

Project element	included in this project				
	units, beds, or clients	new GSF	renovated GSF	total gross area	total on site or served by project
Special care for persons with dementia	36 beds	38,500		38,500	38,500

ASSISTED LIVING FACILITIES
Dementia-specific assisted living models

Project element	new construction		renovations	
	no. units	typical size	no. units	typical size
One bedroom units	36	275		
Total (all units)	36	275		
Residents' social areas (lounges, dining, and recreation spaces)		5,861		
Medical, healthcare, therapies, and activities spaces		2,813		
Administrative, public, and ancillary support services				630
Service, maintenance, and mechanical areas		6,499		
Total gross area		38,500		

CONSTRUCTION COSTS

The following information is based on actual costs

Financing sources: non-taxable bond offering

Building costs
Total building costs $7.1 M
Site costs
Total site costs $745,645
Total project costs $9.3 M

The Village at Waveny Care Center

Status of project: Completed March 2002
Facility administrator: Jeremy M. Vickers
Owner: Waveny Care Center
Architect: Reese, Lower, Patrick & Scott, Ltd.
Interior designer: Reese, Lower, Patrick & Scott, Ltd.
Landscape architect: Stearns & Wheler, LLC
Structural engineer: Parfitt/Ling
Mechanical engineer: Consolidated Engineers
Electrical engineer: Consolidated Engineers
Civil engineer: Stearns & Wheler, LLC
Contractor: A.P. Construction Company

PROJECT AREAS

Project element	included in this project				
	units, beds, or clients	new GSF	renovated GSF	total gross area	total on site or served by project
Special care for persons with dementia	53	58,500	6,130	64,630	119,130

ASSISTED LIVING FACILITIES
Dementia-specific assisted living models

Project element	new construction		renovations
	no. units	typical size	typical size
Studio units	53	300	
Total (all units)	53	300	
Residents' social areas (lounges, dining, and recreation spaces)			14,010
Medical, healthcare, therapies, and activities spaces			2,048
Administrative, public, and ancillary support services			1,739
Service, maintenance, and mechanical areas			6,754
Total gross area			58,241

CONSTRUCTION COSTS

The following information is based on actual costs
Financing sources: non-taxable bond offering with public contributions

Building costs
Total building costs $10.8 M
Site costs
Total site costs $969,000
Total project costs   **$12.1 M**

Westminster-Canterbury on Chesapeake Bay

Status of project: Completed February 2003
Facility administrator: Erle Marie Latimer
Owner: Westminster–Canterbury on Chesapeake Bay
Architect: SFCS Inc.
Interior designer: Design Purchase Link
Landscape architect: Mahan Rykiel Associates, Inc.
Structural engineer: Abiouness, Cross & Bradshaw, Inc.
Mechanical engineer: SFCS Inc.
Electrical engineer: SFCS Inc.
Civil engineer: Landmark Design Group
Contractor: W.M. Jordan Company

PROJECT AREAS

Project element	included in this project				
	units, beds, or clients	new GSF	renovated GSF	total gross area	total on site or served by project
Apartments (units)	164	164		290,000	164
Senior living/assisted living/personal care (units)	91	91		note 1	91
Special care for persons with dementia	14		4,400	4,400	4,400
Skilled nursing care (beds)	72		22,464	22,464	22,464
Common social areas (people)		25,000	10,500	35,500	
Kitchen (daily meals served)	1,141				
Retail space (shops/restaurants, etc)	note 2				
Fitness/rehab/wellness (daily visits)	note 2				
Pool(s) and related areas (users)	note 2				

Note 1: Not applicable—partial renovation and conversion of existing units
Note 2: Listed under 'other facilities'

RESIDENTIAL FACILITIES

Project element	apartments		
	no.	typical size GSF	size range GSF
One bedroom units	37	1,100	1,009–1,125
Two bedroom units	35	1,190	1,190
Two bedroom plus den units	95	1,650	1,427–1,841
Total (all units)	164		
Residents' social areas (lounges, dining, and recreation spaces)		74,950	
Administrative, public, and ancillary support service areas		4,700	
Service, maintenance, and mechanical areas		6,000	
Total gross area		320,000	

ASSISTED LIVING FACILITIES
General social/residential assisted living models

Project element	renovations	
	no. units	typical size
Studio units	56	note 3

Note 3: Size varies. Existing studio-style apartments converted to 'light' assisted living.

Dementia-specific assisted living models

Project element	renovations	
	no. units	typical size
Studio units	14	286
Total (all units)	14	286
Residents' social areas (lounges, dining, and recreation spaces)		1,320
Medical, healthcare, therapies, and activities spaces		500
Administrative, public, and ancillary support services		200
Total gross area		7,040

Medical assisted living models—3rd floor AL

Project element	renovations	
	no. units	typical size
Single occupancy units	21	288
Total (all units)	21	288
Residents' social areas (lounges, dining, and recreation spaces)		750
Medical, healthcare, therapies, and activities spaces		100
Administrative, public, and ancillary support services		100
Total gross area		note 4
Note 4: partial renovations, not applicable		

NURSING FACILITIES

Skilled nursing facilities

Project element	renovations	
	no. beds	typical room size GSF
Residents in one-bed/single rooms	45	287
Residents in two-bed/double rooms	12	360
Social areas (lounges, dining, and recreation spaces)	1,200	
Medical, healthcare, therapies, and activities spaces		140
Administrative, public, and ancillary support services		200
Total gross area		note 5
Note 5: partial renovations, not applicable		

OTHER FACILITIES

Community center

Project element	new construction		renovations	
	no.	size GSF	no.	size GSF
Wellness/Fitness/Pool	1	8,000		
Chapel	1	3,200		
Arts/Crafts	1	2,300		
Barber/Beauty	1	1,200		
Multipurpose	1	6,000		
Wood shop	1	800		
Clinic	1	3,700		
PT/OT	1	1,300		
Service, maintenance and mechanical areas				2,250
Total gross area,				note 6
Note 6: partial renovations, not applicable				

CONSTRUCTION COSTS

The following information is based on actual costs

Final construction cost as of February 2003

Financing sources: non-taxable bond offering

Building costs

Total building costs $56.1 M

Site costs

Total site costs $1.7 M

Total project costs $60.5 M

WESTMINSTER-CANTERBURY, INC.

Status of project: Completed April 2003
Facility administrator: Hunsdon Cary, III
Owner: Westminster–Canterbury, Inc.
Architect–campus expansion & wellness center: SFCS Inc.
Interior designer–campus expansion: GMK Associates
Landscape architect–campus expansion: Proctor Harvey
Landscape architect–wellness center: Hurt & Proffit, Inc.
Structural engineer–campus expansion: SFCS Inc.
Mechanical engineer–campus expansion: SFCS Inc.
Electrical engineer–campus expansion: SFCS Inc.
Civil engineer–campus expansion: SFCS Inc.
Structural engineer–wellness center: SFCS Inc.
Mechanical engineer–wellness center: Kincaid–Jennings
Electrical engineer–wellness center: Kincaid–Jennings
Civil engineer–wellness center: Hurt & Proffit, Inc.
Contractor–campus expansion: W.M. Jordan Company
Contractor–wellness center: C.L. Lewis & Company, Inc.

PROJECT AREAS

Project element	included in this project				
	units, beds, or clients	new GSF	renovated GSF	total gross area	total on site or served by project
Apartments (units)	56	83,008	9,392	92,400	92,400
Special care for persons with dementia	14	9,100		9,100	9,100
Common social areas (people)		14,000	27,000	41,000	41,000
Kitchen (daily meals served)	800	1,000	600	1,600	1,600
Fitness/rehab/wellness (daily visits)		1,300	3,000	4,100	4,100
Pool(s) and related areas (users)		7,400		7,200	7,200
One serving pantry for memory-care unit					200
Two renovated pantries for healthcare					300 each

RESIDENTIAL FACILITIES

Project element	apartments		
	no.	typical size GSF	size range GSF
One bedroom units	32	1,000	700–1,000
Two bedroom units	6	1,300	1,300–1,400
Two bedroom plus den units	18	1,350	1,350–1,475
Total (all units)	56		66,643
Residents' social areas (lounges)			1,500
Service, maintenance, and mechanical areas			5,200
Total gross area			92,400

ASSISTED LIVING FACILITIES

Dementia-specific assisted living models

Project element	new construction		renovations
	no.units	typical size GSF	typical size GSF
Studio units	14	300	
Total (all units)	14	4,200	
Residents' social areas (lounges, dining, and recreation spaces)			3,500
Medical, healthcare, therapies, and activities spaces			1,000
Administrative, public, and ancillary support services			350
Service, maintenance, and mechanical areas			50
Total gross area			9,100

OTHER FACILITIES

Project element	new construction		renovations
	no.	size GSF	size GSF
Wellness/fitness center	1	4,000	
Medical/dental exam/clinic			2,400
Social areas (lounges, dining, and recreation spaces)		1,300	
Administrative, public, and ancillary support services		1,100	
Service, maintenance, and mechanical areas		1,000	
Total gross area			11,300

CONSTRUCTION COSTS

The following information is based on actual costs

Final construction cost as of April 2003

Financing sources: non-taxable bond offering

Building costs

Total building costs — $18.9 M

Site costs

Total site costs — $1.2 M

Total project costs — **$20.1 M**

WILLIAMSBURG LANDING, EDGEWOOD EXPANSION

Status of project: Estimated completion date October 2006
Facility administrator: William Doig, Executive Director
Owner: Williamsburg Landing
Architect: Cochran, Stephenson & Donkervoet, Inc.
Interior designer: Cochran, Stephenson & Donkervoet, Inc.
Landscape architect: Mahan Rykiel Associates, Inc.
Structural engineer: Morabito Consultants, Inc.
Mechanical engineer: James Posey Associates, Inc.
Electrical engineer: James Posey Associates, Inc.
Civil engineer: Landmark Design Group
Contractor: W.M. Jordan Company

PROJECT AREAS

Project element	included in this project				
	units, beds, or clients	new GSF	renovated GSF	total gross area	total on site or served by project
Apartments (units)	31	70,140		70,140	
Cottages/villas (units)	32	77,925		77,925	
Fitness/rehab/wellness (daily visits)		20,185		24,580	
Pool(s) and related areas (users)included in		4,395		24,580	

RESIDENTIAL FACILITIES

Project element	cottages			apartments		
	no.	typical size GSF	size range GSF	no.	typical size GSF	size range GSF
Two bedroom plus den units	27	2,400	2,200–2,600	31	1,850	1,810–1,900
Three bedroom and larger units	5	2,620	2,620			
Total (all units)	32	77,925		31	70,140	
Residents' social areas (lounges, dining, and recreation spaces)					2,750	
Administrative, public, and ancillary support service areas (garage)					21,257	
Service, maintenance, and mechanical areas					600	
Total gross area					113,170	

OTHER FACILITIES

Project element	new construction	
	no.	size GSF
Wellness and fitness center	1	24,580
Social areas (lounges, dining, and recreation spaces)		15,122
Administrative, public, and ancillary support services		1,149
Service, maintenance, and mechanical areas		2,073
Total gross area		24,580

CONSTRUCTION COSTS

The following information is based on bids

Financing sources: non-taxable bond offering

Building costs

Total building costs — $21.8 M

Site costs

Total site costs — $2.2 M

Total project costs — **Not known**

Willow Valley Cultural Center

Status of project: Completed 2002
Facility administrator: Britt Mills
Owner: Willow Valley Retirement Communities
Architect: Bernardon Haber Holloway Architects PC
Interior designer: Design for Functional Interiors
Structural engineer: Baker, Ingram & Associates
Mechanical engineer: Clark, Inc.
Electrical engineer: Clark, Inc.
Civil engineer: RGS Associates, Inc
Consultant: Protech Mechanical Contractors ^ Plumbing & Fire Protection
Contractor: Paul Risk Associates, Inc.

CONSTRUCTION COSTS
Total project costs $9.1 M

Index of Architects

INDEX OF PROJECTS